Praise for *Trust Your Canary*

"*Trust Your Canary* is an indispensable tool for organizational leaders at all levels. It educates readers about the latest research and also provides practical, easy-to-remember strategies to build skills and prevent and address incivility in all its manifestations. Sharone Bar-David is a leading authority on the topic who also understands the legal frameworks that protect employees and the practical challenges that face workplace leaders day to day. This is a book you'll want to refer to again and again."

—**DAVID A. WRIGHT**, Chair, Law Society Tribunal; former associate chair, Human Rights Tribunal of Ontario

"A must-have for the management bookshelf! *Trust Your Canary* combines knowledge about incivility and workplace abuse with highly practical ideas on tackling these issues inside organizations. It is ideal for managers and professionals involved in changing workplace behavior widely, and those working with difficult individuals and teams. It guides the creation of the business case for action and provides excellent advice on strategies to effect change."

—**PROF. CHARLOTTE RAYNER**, Portsmouth Business School, University of Portsmouth; past president, International Association on Workplace Bullying and Harassment

"In *Trust Your Canary*, Sharone Bar-David opens our eyes to the frequent and devastating incidences of workplace incivility: why it happens, how it happens, and the effects it has on the worker, the workplace, organizational climate and productivity. In a highly readable and engaging style, she also provides innovative strategies for what can be done about it. This is an important book for managers, organizational decision makers and union representatives."

—**KIPLING D. WILLIAMS**, Professor, Department of Psychological Sciences, Purdue University; author of *Ostracism: The Power of Silence*

"Sharone Bar-David offers a comprehensive approach to what leaders need to know to establish and maintain a civil work culture. High performance teams require 'high civility' interactions, and Bar-David offers a full array of specific strategies to achieve this."

—DR. LAURA CRAWSHAW, author of *Taming the Abrasive Manager*, Founder and Director of The Boss Whispering Institute

"Sharone Bar-David has created a tremendously insightful resource that should be widely read. With increased attention focused on workplace incivility, bullying and harassment as a result of high-profile scandals, employers and individuals need to understand their rights and obligations. They must also recognize incivility in the workplace and how, left unchecked, it can lead to bullying. *Trust Your Canary* should help to reduce the number of allegations of bullying and harassment that come across my desk."

—STUART E. RUDNER, Rudner MacDonald LLP

Trust Your Canary

SHARONE BAR-DAVID

TRUST
..... your .....
CANARY

Every Leader's Guide to
Taming Workplace Incivility

Copyright © 2015 by Sharone Bar-David

All rights reserved. No part of this book may be reproduced, stored in a retrieval system or transmitted, in any form or by any means, without the prior written consent of the publisher or a licence from The Canadian Copyright Licensing Agency (Access Copyright). For a copyright licence, visit www.accesscopyright.ca or call toll free to 1-800-893-5777.

Fairleigh Press
Toronto, Canada

Cataloguing data available from Library and Archives Canada

ISBN 978-0-9947264-0-7 (paperback)
ISBN 978-0-9947264-1-4 (ebook)

Cover and text design by Kevan D'Agostino
Typesetting by Nayeli Jimenez
Canary image by Dejana Erich

15 16 17 18 19   5 4 3 2 1

All references to people or workplace events in this book have been changed to protect the privacy of those involved.

Ever since the 1896 Tylorstown pit disaster in Wales, coalmine workers would carry caged canaries down into the dark tunnels with them.

The canaries would chirp happily as long as the air was clear and safe.

But if dangerous gases got released within the mineshaft, the canaries would die, their death alerting the miners to the presence of deadly danger.

Inside every one of us resides our own personal canary.

Its purpose is to alert us when the invisible line between civil and uncivil behavior has been crossed.

WHO SHOULD READ THIS BOOK?

You will find this book particularly useful if you are:

- An experienced leader in roles such as director, manager, supervisor or team leader
- New to leadership and want to get it right from the get-go
- A project manager who is directly involved in managing people
- A human resources or organizational development professional, employee relations or diversity expert
- A leader who wants to lead a high-performance team
- A leader dealing with ongoing, dysfunctional team dynamics that don't seem to go away
- A leader who wants to be inspiring and effective but instead is bogged down by having to deal with petty behaviors
- A leader who is aware of increasing accountability requirements related to human rights, regulators' requirements and collective agreements

… And anyone who has an interest in understanding workplace incivility or taming it.

CONTENTS

Foreword · *xv*

Acknowledgments · *xvii*

Introduction · *xix*

The 50–50 Deal, or the Best Way to Approach the Book's Ideas · *xxii*

PART 1 THE PROBLEM AND ITS SYMPTOMS · 1

1 What Is Workplace Incivility? · 3

Defining Workplace Incivility · 3

The Real-Life Manifestations of Workplace Incivility · 7

Why Civility Matters in the First Place · 15

An Under-the-Radar, Undiagnosed Disease · 17

States of Incivility Disease: A Typology · 21

Incivility, Harassment and Bullying · 24

Invisible Culprits: Organizational Change and Personal Stress Levels · 31

2 The Effects of Incivility on Individuals · 33

Real-Life Reactions to Workplace Incivility · 33

Teflon or Velcro: The Two Main Reactions to Incivility · 35

Motivation and Ability · 37

What the Research Tells Us · 38

Guerilla Warfare on the Job, or the Spiral Effect · 42

3 How Incivility Affects Teams, Organizational Indicators and Customer Service · *49*

    Team Effects · *50*

    Customer Service · *52*

    Impact on Innovation · *55*

    Retention, Commitment, Engagement · *55*

    Why Such Extreme Responses to Incivility? · *58*

4 Why Incivility Persists Despite the Damage It Creates · *65*

    Not Connecting the Dots · *66*

    Weak or Nonexistent Organizational Values · *67*

    Ineffective Organizational Processes and Solutions · *69*

    Uncivil Organizational Culture · *71*

    Incivility at the Top · *73*

    Leaders' Omissions, Mistakes and Oversights · *75*

    Management-Union Issues · *81*

5 Blinding Beliefs that Enable Incivility · *85*

    Underlying Beliefs and Workplace Incivility · *85*

    Six Beliefs to Watch For · *86*

What Works? · *96*

PART 2 STRATEGIES AND SOLUTIONS · *99*

6 Mind the Broken Windows: A Foundational Philosophy · *101*

    What Do Broken Windows and Incivility Have in Common? · *101*

    Fixing Windows in Australian Army Style · *105*

    Organizational Window-Fortifying Strategies · *107*

    When the Senior Leaders Are the Obstacles to Minding the Windows · *111*

7 It All Begins with You: Walk the Talk · 121

Incivility and Power · 122

The Self-Examination Imperative · 124

Manage Your Stress Levels · 132

Defensive Management in a World Saturated with Harassment and Bullying · 134

Lead with a Focus on Perceived Justice · 137

8 Know When the Line Is Crossed: Trust Your Canary, and a Civility Litmus Test · 143

Canaries in Our Midst · 144

An Activated Canary Means Action · 146

A World of Ever-Shifting Lines and Banners · 149

Raise the Banner: A Civility Litmus Test · 152

9 Tools of the Trade: Screwdrivers at Your Disposal · 159

Getting the Support You Need · 159

What to Do: Action Planning Criteria · 164

10 Provide Corrective Feedback: Follow the S-B-D Method · 169

In Praise of a Solid Structure · 169

Two Useful Strategies to Increase the Chances of Success · 170

The S-B-D Feedback Method, Step-by-Step · 173

Pulling the S-B-D Feedback Together · 182

11 Go Public: Handling Situations that Happen in Front of Others · 187

The Imperative to Respond in Public · 187

Barriers to Responding in Public · 190

Mistakes to Avoid · 192

Objectives and Considerations When You Go Public · 193

Going Public, Step-by-Step · 195

12 Making Everyone Care: Create a Civil Team Culture · 201

Taking Action to Boost Team Civility · 201

Prevention and Maintenance Touchstones · 202

Dealing with Chronic Team Incivility · 212

13 Down in the Trenches: Dealing with Chronically Uncivil Individuals · 221

It's Time to Step Up and Deal with It · 221

Before All Else: Own Management's Contribution to the Problem · 224

Doing It, Step-by-Step · 227

But What if Nothing Changes? · 234

14 Action on the Ground: Know Exactly What to Say, How and When · 239

Choices, Choices and More Choices · 239

Mixing and Matching Verbal Interventions · 247

Verbal Responses to Avoid · 248

15 Dealing with Incivility that Is Directed Toward You · 261

Incivility from Colleagues · 216

Incivility from Staff · 264

Incivility from Your Manager · 266

Incivility from a Union Representative · 271

16 Make It Happen: Where to Go from Here · 277

Preparation, Action, Success · 277

Build Civility into the Team's DNA · 284

The Road Ahead · 285

Conclusion · 289

Endnotes · 291

TABLES

1 Leaders' Thinking Errors · 19
2 *Canadian HR Reporter* Survey: Negative Impact of Incivility on Key Organizational Indicators · 57
3 The S-O-S System · 113
4 Intentions-Perceptions Traps · 126
5 Behaviors to Avoid · 131
6 Bully Bosses in the Media · 135
7 The S-B-D Method · 175
8 Checklist: Preparing for the Meeting · 183
9 Scanning Tool for Team Civility · 203
10 Barriers to Changing a Chronically Uncivil Team Culture · 215
11 Verbal Intervention Options · 240

FOREWORD

....

When I think of incivility, I think of Sharone.

Not because she's an uncivil person—she's about the furthest thing from it. But rather because I have yet to encounter a better authority on the topic of abrasive behavior in my many years as a journalist covering the workplace.

She has written or collaborated on more than thirty articles found in *Canadian HR Reporter* over the last decade. She was instrumental in putting together a groundbreaking national survey of HR professionals, the results of which you will find throughout these pages.

On paper, there's no better person to write this book. But we all know that "on paper" often means nothing. As impressive as Sharone's credentials are, it's not why I agreed to write this foreword. It's not why, when the CBC or other news agencies phone me looking for an expert, I hand over her phone number without hesitation.

The reason I do all that—collaborate with and publish Sharone, as well as refer her to others—is because of the conversations we've had since I first met her at an HR conference in 2008. What impresses me so much, and why I admire and respect her work, is how quick she is on her feet. If I have a problem, I'll bounce it off her and, without a moment's hesitation, out comes the perfect answer, the perfect solution, the best way to address the problem. Every single time.

And the issue of incivility and respect in the workplace is one that needs to be addressed. We have all seen what happens to workplaces when bullies are left unchecked. Low morale, decreased productivity and increased turnover. It's a recipe for failure, and it all hinges on leaders' ability to take action well before such behavior escalates.

Managing incivility isn't a nice-to-have soft skill, not in this day and age when we see countless headlines related to misbehaving employees and the employers who turned a blind eye. Harassment and bullying are far more than just taboo productivity killers—they're illegal. They carry significant legal liabilities, and jurisdiction after jurisdiction has added psychological harassment to health and safety legislation in recent years. Employers and managers who know how to keep incivility at bay can avoid such liabilities.

Sharone knows incivility inside out, knows the damage it causes and—most importantly—how to disarm it. Her advice will make you a better leader, help you get more out of your teams and create a working environment where everyone can thrive.

TODD HUMBER
Associate Publisher/Managing Editor
Canadian HR Reporter
Thomson Reuters

ACKNOWLEDGMENTS

∙∙∙∙∙∙∙∙∙∙∙∙∙∙∙∙∙∙∙∙∙∙∙∙

Heartfelt thanks to the thousands of people who have participated in my workshops, keynote speeches, coaching and consulting engagements, and who were willing to join me on the journey of developing my ideas, testing them out through (sometimes feisty) discussions, and who were willing to laugh together and struggle together as we collaboratively walked the path toward making us all more civil and respectful, and then creating workplaces that strived to be so too.

And a deep thank-you to those whose unrelenting support helped me get my ideas from inside my head and from those training and consulting spaces into this book. To Geraldine Ryan, who over a delightful Christmas lunch in 2012 relentlessly insisted that I "absolutely had to" share my ideas with the world. To Judi Hughes of Your Planning Partners, whose well of wisdom and patient support carried the day from inception to completion. To people who have walked the author's path and generously shared their experiences: Gil Broza, Randal Craig, Andrea Zanetti and Jennifer Black. To my friends and colleagues Karon West and Liza Provenzano, who provided thoughtful commentary on some organizational development and human resources segments of the book. To my clients over the past year, who endured days of me being incommunicado during the writing process and whose belief in the project helped keep me going.

To my family in Canada and overseas who couldn't wait to see the book published and reminded me that I am walking in my parents' footsteps: my mother, Molly Lyons Bar-David, a prolific author whose typewriter was always clicking in the background, and my father, Yaap Bar-David, whose love of books fueled his career as a literary agent.

A special thank-you to the professionals who spend their lives in the publishing business helping people like me get it right: to my editor, Karen Milner, whose feedback and sharp grasp of the issues gave me the confidence to stand proudly behind this book. Heartfelt thanks to editor Catherine Leek; your sage input and commonsense advice in the first phases of the project were invaluable. To proofreader Judy Phillips, whose editorial meticulousness and considerable visual sensibilities delivered the manuscript safely to its final form. To Jesse Finkelstein at Page Two, who ever so competently oversaw the process of transforming the manuscript into a real-life book with equanimity, strategic thinking, empathy and exquisite expertise.

And finally, to the two who were the closest to me and the project throughout: my magnificent daughter, Leore, who patiently endured those times when I was unavailable to her and continuously expressed her belief in her mother's success. And to Rob, my wonderful partner, whose unabashed pride, emotional support and editorial input have been a constant throughout. Without the two of you, this book would not have been a reality.

Thanks to you all.

SHARONE BAR-DAVID
Toronto, April 2015

INTRODUCTION

If you've picked up this book, I venture to guess that you have identified a problem in your work environment. Perhaps you encounter rude or discourteous interpersonal exchanges on the team that you lead and you are at a loss as to what to do about this negative behavior. Or the problem could be far more subtle. In fact, you may not even be able to pinpoint or label precisely what is wrong, but you sure know that it's getting in the way of high performance and healthy relations.

The problems you see may pop up sporadically or on a regular basis. Perhaps they are even chronic. They trigger within you an uncomfortable gut feeling that leaves you uncertain about how to analyze the situation accurately or what (constructively) to do about it. You may be a veteran leader or relatively new to leadership, or a senior leader, mid-level manager or frontline supervisor, and still you are at a loss.

You've tried different solutions. Some worked well, some not so much. You've consulted with various people, and the advice ranged from very helpful to, well, not so much. You've tried developing a systematic approach to solving the issue, with mixed results. You are now ready to take meaningful action.

This book might be the answer to your quest. Its sole purpose is to help you boost your skills so that you can accurately assess these uncomfortable situations and then take effective action. With this book in hand, you will be able to boost civility on your team meaningfully and consistently, and become a better leader overall while doing so. When the team you lead is civil and respectful, its members can perform at their best, unencumbered by worry, anxiety or acts of mini-aggression aimed at getting even with an uncivil colleague. They are free to focus and innovate and create because they are not worried about their ideas getting shot down. Productivity, collaboration and teamwork are high, and customer service is, therefore, at its best.

Since the early 1990s, my company, Bar-David Consulting, has been providing training and consulting services to organizations across industries and sectors. Over time, our focus has increasingly shifted to two phenomena that exist in many organizations but tend to get ignored, or are handled ineffectively: workplace incivility and abrasive leadership. Both trigger problems within the work environment and have an adverse effect on the business. Through my training and consulting practice, I have had the opportunity to test which behaviors are problematic across sectors, and I will offer these as examples throughout this book, along with suggested solutions.

This book fills a glaring gap in the current literature. Currently, there is no hands-on, comprehensive resource for leaders to help them navigate the rough waters of workplace incivility with practical strategies that bring their true struggles and reality into account. Every page of this book reflects what I have heard from thousands of managers and serves as my attempt to help you in the most straightforward, easy-to-implement way. Experience has taught me that the more skilled the manager at identifying and dealing with incivility, the less incivility there is on the team. And yet, so many managers lack such skills.

Trying to tame incivility can involve some very difficult, uncomfortable conversations that don't come naturally to managers. And, sadly, many of us are not taught how to deal with these thorny issues in business school or on the job. Even if we are taught to deal with these matters, the execution part is exceedingly challenging. Therefore, in many instances in this book, you will find very specific suggested phrasing laid out to help you handle particularly tricky situations.

The work environment that I invite you to aspire to, and that this book will help you achieve, may seem light years away from where your workplace is now. Maybe you have never experienced anything even remotely close to it. But I can tell you this: Such workplaces do exist, and they depend on leaders like you to make it happen. This book will help move you to create such a workplace, with your current employer or elsewhere.

You will never find a work environment completely free of incivility. Most of us engage in uncivil behavior inadvertently, unintentionally and sometimes even unconsciously. We ignore someone, make a sarcastic comment or use our electronic devices in ways that make others feel dismissed. That is why this book is subtitled "Every leader's guide to taming workplace incivility" and not "Every leader's guide to abolishing incivility." In your role as a leader, you will never be able to eradicate incivility entirely, but you sure can minimize and tame it.

To help you get there, in this book you will find an abundance of information and strategies, including:

- A comprehensive definition of workplace incivility, in all its guises

- A discussion of how incivility affects your people and the business

- An exploration of why incivility persists, despite the damage it leaves in its wake

- Insights on what stops leaders like you from taking effective action

- Dozens of anecdotes that demonstrate how incivility manifests itself and what you as a leader can do to drum it out of your culture

- Dozens of tried-and-true strategies and tips sprinkled throughout the book, complete with step-by-step coaching ideas and samples of specific phrasing, all geared to helping you deal with real-life situations, in real time

- Implementation Clinics that summarize key ideas, accompanied by practical exercises
- A coherent framework for diagnosing and handling incivility

THE 50–50 DEAL, OR THE BEST WAY TO APPROACH THE BOOK'S IDEAS

As you read this book, you may at times find yourself disagreeing with my opinions or recommendations. There might be times when you think that I have completely gone off the deep end of political correctness. You might wonder whether I truly understand how real workplaces operate. Or you might think that I am describing a utopian workplace that never existed and likely never will.

If that's the case, great. It means that we are truly in dialogue, you and me. It means that my ideas are sufficiently provocative to cause you to go deeper into your own thinking, experiences and reality, where you can find your own unique answers, ones that reflect who you are and what you stand for. This place of questioning is where your growth as a leader occurs.

To encourage you to engage with the ideas in this book fully, I'd like to offer you a "50–50 deal." It's a framework that I use with participants in my civility-boosting training workshops, and which has consistently proven to be useful to their learning journey. My hope is that it will serve to enhance your experience, too, as you read this book.

With this deal, I will be responsible for 50 percent of making this book worth your time, and you will be responsible for the other 50 percent. In my 50 percent, I will bring my passion and expertise to this book and do my best to make the ideas accessible and practical. At times, I will be opinionated and put forth positions in a very strong fashion, as though these ideas are the only truth, in black and white with no shades of gray. In these instances, you might find yourself resisting or discounting my views.

And that's where your 50 percent comes in. In your 50 percent, you will commit to considering these strong ideas with an open and fair mind, and then contemplate how they actually fit (or not) with your own thinking, experience and who you are as a leader.

That's it, very simple: I will be opinionated and you will be open-minded.

So, do we have our deal?

PART 1

THE PROBLEM AND ITS SYMPTOMS

....

IN THIS SECTION OF THE BOOK YOU WILL DISCOVER:

- What workplace incivility means and how it manifests in organizations and teams

- What the human brain and body do when they encounter incivility

- The risks associated with not addressing incivility

- How to distinguish between different forms of counterproductive behavior: incivility, harassment and bullying

- The compelling business case related to workplace incivility: its effects on teams, performance and the business itself

- Six top reasons for the persistence of incivility despite the damage it creates

1

WHAT IS WORKPLACE INCIVILITY?

The road got more bumpy, more rocky, more tricky.
By midnight, I tell you, my stomach felt icky.
—Dr. Seuss, *I Had Trouble in Getting to Solla Sollew*

DEFINING WORKPLACE INCIVILITY

Throughout this book, we'll be using the following definition to describe workplace incivility:

Workplace incivility refers to seemingly insignificant behaviors that are rude, disrespectful, discourteous or insensitive, where the intent to harm is ambiguous or unclear.[1]

The first thing you might notice is that this definition is somewhat vague. It may not be as concrete and satisfying as you would like it to be. In fact, several aspects of this definition are ambiguous and highly subjective. For example, what constitutes a "rude" or "seemingly insignificant" behavior will vary greatly from one person to another, and even from one team to another. (No worries, we will discuss many of these issues throughout the book so that you can move forward with clarity.)

Let's look at the various elements of the definition of workplace incivility. The first part focuses on the seemingly inconsequential, low intensity nature of the behavior. The behaviors in question do not necessarily involve gross offenses or outright insults but, rather, are often minor actions that seem trivial, the kind that anyone can engage in without necessarily even knowing it. They occur within the subtlety of words and actions, where manner and body language set the tone for how the words should be interpreted. Take for example a manager asking an employee, "Have you considered using the new system to solve this problem?" This question, when delivered in a neutral tone, will cause no offense and may, in fact, be perceived as helpful. However, the same words delivered with an emphasis on the words "have you" or "considered," accompanied by an impatient tone, will be perceived as belittling and even humiliating.

The second part focuses on the nature of the behavior itself—"rude and discourteous." This, too, is a relative term. What is acceptable in one culture, team or context may not be as welcome in another, and what a member of one generation considers acceptable can be offensive to a member of a different generation. The range, complexity and subtleties of human interactions cannot be boxed into a hard definition. And yet as a manager you are required to act, even amid ambiguity. In your organization and on your team, much of the determination as to what is rude, discourteous and insensitive will lie in your hands.

The definition's third element focuses on intent to harm—"unclear or ambiguous." In most incivility situations it is exceedingly difficult to determine whether the person intended to harm, offend or hurt. Take for example an instance where a few team members have forged friendships outside work. In the presence of Emily, another colleague who is not part of the friendship circle, they refer to outings they had and they giggle at inside jokes without including Emily. The intent to harm might be unclear, but the effects of this behavior on Emily, especially if repeated over time, might be quite negative. Or consider the case of someone rolling her eyes when a colleague is speaking—it is hard to determine whether this is an innocent expression of frustration or an intentional dismissive move.

Furthermore, many of the behaviors that we will refer to as uncivil are associated with certain commonly accepted personality traits. For example, some people are considered by themselves (and others) to be straight shooters, or sarcastic or moody and, as such, they might engage in behaviors that the person on the receiving end may experiences as outright rude, disrespectful or hurtful. In these cases the intent to harm is unclear, but the impact is deeply felt.

Some uncivil behaviors are highly personal, whereas others are victimless. The first category refers to actions that are clearly directed at a specific person or persons. Under this class you will find behaviors such as gossiping about a coworker, snickering when a colleague is delivering a presentation, or making a belittling comment about someone's skills. These highly personal behaviors can also take place via electronic or computer means, such as sending a critical email to a person with others copied on the communication.

The victimless behaviors, on the other hand, comprise inconsiderate conduct that is not directed at a specific person or group of people. Here you will find behaviors such as carrying on a loud conversation in an open-concept work environment, or leaving the lunchroom microwave dirty when others need to use it. These are bad habits but they (usually) are not likely to trigger the strong types of reactions that the personal type of incivility will create. I classify these behaviors as unprofessional rather than uncivil because they violate what most people would consider to be the norms of good judgment and workplace courtesy.[2]

The lines between unprofessional behavior and uncivil behavior are blurry. For example, if someone continues to have a loud conversation in an open workspace even if asked to stop because it interrupts other people's work, then this behavior would now be classified as uncivil: The person who is doing this now knows full well that others are bothered but still continues to do it.

Throughout this book, we will be focusing on the first type of incivility, which is more personal in nature. These behaviors cause the most turmoil and have the greatest implications for people, teams and the work itself. They are also the ones that you as a leader will find more challenging to diagnose and handle and where you are more likely to make mistakes that will lead to negative ramifications. As to the uncivil behaviors of the more unprofessional kind, you can implement relatively simple measures to deal effectively with those, even when they tend to be persistent or when initiated by chronic offenders. In fact, you will find that you can readily apply most of the strategies in this book to such situations as well.

So how do you navigate your way through all this ambiguity? The good news is that in addition to everything this book will help you learn to do, you can always rely on your "inner canary"—a built-in human alarm system akin to the canaries that coal miners would take into the tunnels to alert them of the presence of poisonous gases. When you witness incivility, this canary gets activated. It manifests in the form of a strong inner sensation that tells you that something isn't quite right. (It's a "gut feeling" of sorts.) It may come as a physical sensation, such as a pang in your stomach, or an overwhelming sense of discomfort that suddenly descends upon you. Sometimes it may come in the form of a thought, such as "Wow, that was super rude." While you may not be able to pinpoint exactly what is bothering you, you intuitively sense that something about the situation isn't right. In chapter 8 we will delve more deeply into how you can best use your canary, but for now, I hope you find comfort in knowing that your own personal alert is there to aid you in a very real way—once you learn to trust it.

THE REAL-LIFE MANIFESTATIONS OF WORKPLACE INCIVILITY

Molly, my sister, and I fell out,
And what do you think it was all about?
She loved coffee and I loved tea
And that was the reason we couldn't agree.
—Mother Goose, "Coffee and Tea"

Any attempt to capture the full range of behaviors that qualify as workplace incivility would require more pages than the covers of a single book can contain. They range from barely visible behavior right up to blatantly rude conduct that verges on harassment. As you read the list of common uncivil behaviors that follows, you might be struck by how seemingly insignificant many of them seem. You might think that people should know better than to behave in these ways or, conversely, that those on the receiving end shouldn't take such minor infractions to heart. And yet, your own experience might already have taught you that whether or not you approve of it, the reality is that people do get offended, upset and even retaliatory when they experience these behaviors from a colleague or manager. As you read further into this book, you will discover fascinating statistics about the far-reaching effects that these small acts have on people, performance, engagement and teamwork.

As you go through the examples of common, uncivil behaviors included below, I invite you to ask yourself which of these behaviors you have personally demonstrated (maybe even for a good reason, or at least that's what you told yourself), perhaps even as recently as within the past week. If you can't find at least one or two examples, extend the search period to two weeks. You should be able to find examples where other people would consider your behavior to be uncivil, even if only in a small way.

- **No hellos, skipping greetings.** There's something about skipping this basic nicety that really gets under people's skin and causes them to be resentful and retaliatory. In fact, in our civility-boosting training programs, we present the definition of incivility and then ask participants to brainstorm examples of behaviors that fit the definition. In the vast majority of cases, greeting-related issues come up as one of the first two examples cited by participants. No wonder: you've probably heard salutation-related complaints more than once and may have felt incredulous at how childish it seems to care about this, let alone complain to a manager. Stay tuned for the section about ostracism, where we will explore why such seemingly insignificant behavior triggers so much upset.

- **Eye-rolling.** Eye-rolling is a highly potent dismissive act that takes a nanosecond to execute. Because of its nonverbal yet aggressive nature, most people feel unable to respond to it, or at least to do so in a constructive fashion. Instead, they engage in mini-retaliatory acts. No wonder that eye-rolling is the second most frequently mentioned example of workplace incivility by our sessions' participants.

- **Belittling of opinions, experience and skills.** Belittling of another person can be expressed through words, tone or the body language that accompanies otherwise neutral words. It can happen in private or in public, but a public reprimand or belittling—especially from a person of authority—tends to add a layer of humiliation and upset. Note that when a manager engages in these behaviors, the impact tends to be significantly greater than when it happens between colleagues.

    The line between legitimate feedback and belittling is easy to cross. People have varying levels of sensitivity to challenging feedback, and what may be perceived by one person as helpful can be painfully stinging to another.

- **Talking down.** Speaking to someone in a condescending or over-simplified manner, as if they don't know much, is a specific form of belittling. It can be done in a seemingly kind way, but the condescending delivery of the content sends a strong—and upsetting—message that the person at the receiving end is perceived as incompetent.

- **Sarcasm.** The dictionary defines sarcasm as "the use of irony to mock or convey contempt." Sarcasm often manifests when a person seems to praise something or someone but is instead cutting or taunting. It can be as simple as responding to a person's mistake by saying, "Oh, that was really well done!" or responding to someone expressing an idea with, "No! Really? You're so smart!" Some people practice sarcasm on a regular basis and even pride themselves on having a sarcastic personality, thinking that this form of expression is clever or funny, or makes them more interesting. But there's nothing amusing or interesting about being on the receiving end of a pointed, sarcastic comment. Instead, it is experienced as incivility.

- **Gossip.** Gossip involves unflattering conversation about another person's behavior or affairs that would make that person feel uncomfortable or upset if they were to hear it. Gossip ranges from a relatively benign discussion to spreading false rumors. It is exceedingly difficult to know when a legitimate, sometimes even work-focused, discussion about a colleague has morphed into a gossipy conversation.

  Gossip in the workplace is frequently legitimized when it is classified as venting. You, too, may have shared your frustration and upset about a colleague or a situation with another colleague without pausing to consider that your conversation has shifted from appropriate advice-seeking to gossip, which would be hurtful to the other person were they to hear it.

- **Cliques, social exclusion, shutting someone out.** In the complexities of human interaction, it is difficult to ascertain where on-the-job friendships are constructive and desirable and where they begin to marginalize and exclude those who are not part of those relationships. As a leader, it is challenging to handle those ambiguous situations where, on a regular basis, several colleagues are having lots of fun going out to lunch while they clearly leave another colleague behind. You do not feel it is your place as manager to tell people whom they should socialize with, yet you see the formation of clear lines of exclusion on your team. True, some people like to be left alone and do not seek extra social interaction on the job; however, as a manager you still need to ensure that these people are not feeling ignored or disregarded. As you will see later on, such experiences impede people's ability to perform their job.

- **Dismissive, excluding or judgmental body language.** In this category you will find a vast array of behaviors, including finger pointing, turning one's back away, giving someone a dirty look, various hand gestures, shrugged shoulders, facial expressions, raised eyebrows—you name it and someone has used their body in some creative way to express disapproval, contempt or dismissal. From a leader's perspective, it is challenging to address uncivil behavior that is expressed through body language because many of these gestures defy exact description and because they happen in such a fleeting and often quiet fashion.

- **Dismissive sounds.** Contemptuous sounds are a class unto themselves. If you work in an environment where people use sounds in a way that others perceive as offensive, then you already know how even one such small sound can be worth a thousand dismissive words. Hissing, lip smacking and deep sighs are typical examples of this category. In some work environments, this particular form of incivility is widely practiced, while in others it is rarely present.

- **Interrupting, intruding on boundaries.** Barging into someone's workspace, interrupting formal or informal meetings, using someone's equipment and not returning it, using a person's space and not restoring it to its original state, hovering impatiently over a person to get his or her attention—all these are experienced by people as an uncivil invasion into personal territory. When the offender has a tendency to engage in these behaviors regularly, you can reliably predict that retaliatory acts (sometimes in the form of complaining to other people behind that person's back) will follow.

- **Rude use of technology.** Using mobile devices in the middle of a conversation, emailing in meetings while someone else is presenting or speaking, and continuing to work away on one's computer while in conversation or while on a call—all these qualify as "RUT," or Rude Use of Technology. While one person is engaging in techno-RUT, the others are getting into a reactive relationship-rut.

- **Raised voice.** Most people consider a raised voice or yelling as uncivil. It is belittling and clearly crosses the boundary of what most people would consider as acceptable behavior in the workplace. This is especially true when the offender is a person holding institutional power.

- **Silent treatment.** The opposite of a raised voice, this behavior can be just as upsetting. It involves not speaking to someone altogether, usually over an extended period of time, or speaking with them only for the minimal necessities of performing job-related tasks. Giving someone the silent treatment is a time-honored tradition that crosses cultures and ages. It speaks volumes about shunning the other person—without uttering a word.

- **Passing blame for mistakes onto others.** Mistakes are part of life, and some people are better than others at acknowledging and owning them. But when a person blames someone else for a mistake that they themselves have made, or points a blaming finger at someone for a team blunder, the person at the receiving end will feel unjustly accused.

- **Stealing ideas and taking credit.** Most people feel strongly attached to their ideas and want to be credited for them. When someone else takes credit for a thought or piece of work, the person whose idea it was experiences that as pure theft.

- **Speaking a foreign language in the presence of people who don't understand that language.** The thorny issue of speaking a second language comes up repeatedly (and fiercely) in my work across sectors. When people speak another language in the presence of a colleague who does not speak that language, it triggers exclusion and alienation. In fact, researchers refer to this as "linguistic ostracism."[3]

Most people will tell you that when exposed to such behavior, they have at one point or another—even if only for a fleeting moment—thought this: "Those people are talking about me!" In reality, foreign-language speakers (when being honest) admit that at one point or another they actually had spoken in that language about the unsuspecting person sitting or working right beside them. Maybe they did it only rarely. Maybe they did it only briefly. Maybe it was only a slightly dismissive comment. But they sure did it.

- **Arriving late when others rely on you coming on time.** When Doreen is late to an important client meeting where she has to make an important sales presentation, her colleague Aaron, who has to wait for her, perceives the behavior to be discourteous and disrespectful. The stronger the reliance on the other person arriving on time, the more intense the reaction will be when that person is late.

- **Withholding information.** Sometimes people do not provide information that a colleague needs to perform the job. Many use this particular behavior as a way of getting even with someone whose behavior they consider to be uncivil. They feign forgetfulness and can get away with this behavior without serious ramifications.

- **Use of profanity or swear words.** In some industries or organizations, profanities are accepted as a legitimate form of self-expression—they are not considered to be uncivil. In other workplaces, however, using a swear word sticks out like a sore thumb. It is offensive and even upsetting to those who hear it.

- **Asking for input and then ignoring it.** When one person invites input from another, the person being asked naturally assumes that the input will be incorporated into the matter at hand. When this does not happen and the contribution is ignored, the contributor's basic sense of fairness is violated. This person will feel that the other has taken advantage of him or her and will consider that colleague disrespectful and exploitative.

- **Side conversations during business meetings and presentations.** We've all done it, that little chitchat or comment to a colleague sitting beside us while someone else is presenting, or speaking at a meeting. This side conversation may or may not be related to the topic that the other colleague is speaking about, and to those engaged in the conversation it seems innocent and maybe even fun. But the person who is speaking or presenting experiences the behavior as anywhere from rude to outright humiliating.

- **"That's just who I am" attitude.** This form of incivility occurs when someone has a personality that is rough around the edges, or consistently moody, impatient or condescending. Efforts to provide this person with feedback on his or her behavior are met with a "Well, that's just who I am, take it or leave it." Meanwhile, this person's personality is perceived by others as rude, discourteous and disrespectful, and disrupts the workplace environment. Later in this book, we will address the various traps that managers fall into when they deal with the "that's who I am" form of incivility.

As you may have noticed, it is easy and even human to engage in these behaviors unintentionally and without being aware that one is doing something that affects others negatively. Taking myself as an example, it took considerable reflection to realize that some of my own habits could be considered as uncivil. For example, I am a spontaneous and enthusiastic person and when a good idea hits me, I am eager to share it with others—right now, right here. And so, in what I have always perceived to be a charmingly inimitable habit, I would barge into conversations and physical spaces with contagious (at least in my mind) enthusiasm. Over time I realized that the people whose conversation I was interrupting might see my behavior as neither charming nor endearing. In fact, they could easily, and rightfully, perceive it as discourteous and rude. Once I realized that, I put in place measures to minimize the behavior, and when it does still occasionally occur, I mitigate its effects immediately. Self-reflection and a commitment to persist over the long haul are crucial to eradicating uncivil habits.

WHY CIVILITY MATTERS IN THE FIRST PLACE

As you immerse yourself more deeply into the book, you will learn about the extensive damage that incivility leaves in its wake. The business case for civility will become glaringly clear. But before we delve into the complex terrain of its negative effects, let's pause for a moment to highlight why workplace civility actually matters to the success of your business.

To understand the role that civility plays in your ability to achieve team and organizational goals, consider the game of curling. In this sport, a team of players competes against another to slide the maximum number of polished granite stones from one end of a sheet of ice to a target area at the other end of the ice surface. One player tries to get one stone at a time toward its goal, while two other team members accompany the rock with brooms as it slides down the ice, sweeping the surface constantly to smooth it and allow the stone to move successfully and efficiently to its desired destination.

Civility is the smooth surface that enables your people to perform at their best, leading to best results for the team, the organization and those whom it serves. Your role as the manager is to be the sweeper, the one who ensures that the path is clear (which is exactly what this book is going to help you do). Here are some of the reasons it is crucial that you help people get to the other end, where civility supports organizational and team success:

1. **Performance.** People who are treated with respect are able to focus. Their mind is not bogged down by worry, their brain is not flooded with memory-impeding stress hormones, and their time is not spent on second-guessing whether or not the uncivil person intended to belittle or dismiss them. With focus, they perform at their best.

2. **Trust and teamwork.** Respectful relationships yield trust, and trust makes people support each other in return, collaborate, hold

themselves and one another accountable, be flexible, lend a helping hand, deal effectively with interpersonal problems and work together toward shared goals.

3. **Customer service.** A civil culture within the organization benefits customer service (or patient care, or any third parties relevant to your business). The focus, trust and teamwork that civility brings about result in effective, smooth and cheerful service.

4. **Engagement and retention.** Employees who feel that the organization treats them with respect and that its managers are actively ensuring that everyone is dealt with in a civil manner are willing to give more and are highly invested in the success of the enterprise. They are less likely to depart prematurely.

5. **Innovation.** Innovation relies on people's sense of safety and trust. A civil work environment creates a milieu where new (and possibly unconventional) ideas can be shared and explored without fear.

6. **Health and safety.** A respectful work environment is a psychologically safe one. In a world of ever-growing rates of mental illness on the job, a civil culture prevents the triggering or exacerbation of mental health problems (and the associated high levels of absenteeism and benefits costs). Furthermore, focused and calm employees are less likely to engage in hazardous behavior or be involved in workplace accidents.

The advantages of upholding a civil work environment are almost common sense. The above list covers a small segment of the terrain. And yet, surprisingly, incivility continues to exist uninterrupted in most organizations.

AN UNDER-THE-RADAR, UNDIAGNOSED DISEASE

After I had facilitated a session on workplace incivility with the executive team of a 1,800-strong organization, the general manager approached me and shared, "The term 'incivility' really hit the nail on the head. It describes problems in our organization that we've been struggling with for a long time, but never had the right name to describe. We've referred to it as 'interpersonal conflict' and brought in training for that, and we've called it 'interpersonal communication problems' and tried solving it that way. But the problems continue to fester. We always knew that something was missing in how we thought about it. The term 'incivility' is new to me and to our group and it really hits the mark."

Some months later, after more work was done to boost civility across the enterprise, the same GM expressed that "using the incivility framework really helped change our thinking. From there, it was easier to change our overall approach to the issues."

Incivility flies under the organizational radar as an undiagnosed disease. Leaders and human resources departments observe the actual behaviors but (as the general manager quoted above expressed) they lack the terminology and framework with which to address them effectively.

Wherever there are human beings working together, there will be incivility. It's inevitable. These seemingly insignificant and ambiguous behaviors are woven into the ways in which people interact with one another, and, because so much of it happens unintentionally, it does not get classified as a problem that requires addressing. Rather, organizations and leaders perceive it as an integral part of the landscape. Therefore, when someone complains about a matter that seems petty or trivial, such as others not saying hello or eye-rolling, the complaint is overlooked or even frowned upon.

Because it is an invisible phenomenon, there are typically no policies in place to prevent or address workplace incivility. Some organizations do have a code of conduct that attempts to tackle the issue, and some of these codes (though few and far between) are detailed enough to actually enable employees to grasp the required standard and for managers to hold them accountable to it. However, there is only so much you can capture in a policy. All things considered, a policy that states "Thou shalt say hello to everyone within ten feet of thy physical body within the first twenty-two minutes of arriving at work" would not get a warm reception.

Most striking is the fact that organizations are blind to the fundamental relationship between incivility and business outcomes. They refer to incivility-related problems as relationship issues, or as conflict issues or organizational culture issues, instead of labeling them for what they ultimately are: business issues.

If you want to get serious about boosting workplace civility, the first thing you need to do is use a business lens to identify correctly what is going on and the impact it has on the business. But don't limit your thinking to dollars and cents. You should also examine how workplace incivility affects the delivery of your core mission, its impact on employee engagement, brand reputation, talent retention and other relevant business parameters.

Table 1 contrasts examples of commonplace thinking with the more useful "What is it costing the business?" thinking.

What Is Workplace Incivility? | 19

Table 1: Leaders' Thinking Errors

Leaders' Common Thinking	"What Is It Costing the Business?" Thinking
Until their morning caffeine kicks in, my staff members are grumpy. It's just a part of life around here.	Grumpy staff will cause our customers to turn to our competitors, where the staff consistently demonstrates a cheery attitude. Specifically: What would it cost if X number of customers leave us per month?
Our team members are always late to meetings. I've tried everything to tackle it, with no meaningful results.	At an average hourly salary rate of X dollars per person, what is the annual cost to us when this weekly meeting starts ten minutes late?
Two team members haven't been on speaking terms for years. I've tried mediating between them and implementing other solutions too, but there's just too much history for things to change.	What work processes have become skewed or inefficient because of these people not speaking to each other? What dollar amount can I place annually on each such inefficiency? How much (exactly) are unnecessary workarounds costing us? Have we received complaints from internal or external stakeholders that are directly related to this problem? What impact do these complaints have on our reputation?
Frank (a team leader) can be rough around the edges. He's quick to criticize, sometimes in public.	How does Frank's behavior affect turnover on his team? What was the cost of replacing those who left (or might leave)? How does Frank's behavior stifle new ideas and innovation? And how does that affect our ability to compete or to improve the quality of service?

(continued)

Leaders' Common Thinking	"What Is It Costing the Business?" Thinking
We work in a high-pressure environment. It's natural for people to lash out at each other. Sometimes someone runs out of the room because they are so upset.	When an upset nurse spends five minutes in the washroom crying, a patient in severe pain is forced to wait the extra five minutes until she is sufficiently composed to come to his aid. Every aspect of this situation blatantly violates our most fundamental organizational values of Excellence, Compassion, and Human Dignity. *or* Every time someone runs out of the room as a result of a colleague lashing out, or loses their focus or vents about the event with a colleague, actual work is not getting done, or is getting done at an inferior standard. A calculation of the number of events per day per business unit, multiplied by time lost, and then multiplied by average hourly rate, leads to a monetary cost of $X.
People on the team are frustrated with each other. There's lots of eye-rolling. You really can't control this kind of thing.	The bad feelings between team members affect their work in various ways (define or measure the actual impact). People are engaging in the following getting-even actions (list those actions). The dollar value that can be placed on the above behaviors amounts to $X. Has anyone left the company because of this? If so, by losing these people, we also lost (institutional memory, skills, client relationships and the like). With these team dynamics, service delivery has been affected in the following ways (list details).

STATES OF INCIVILITY DISEASE: A TYPOLOGY

Humpty Dumpty sat on a wall,
Humpty Dumpty had a great fall.
All the king's horses and all the king's men
Couldn't put Humpty together again.
—English nursery rhyme

Workplace incivility is not a static phenomenon. Like other diseases, it has predictable, progressive manifestations. Think of it as an ailment with four key states, or symptoms.

State A: Healthy Body

"Hey guys, yesterday when everyone was joking around about my report, I felt uncomfortable. Can we not go there again?"

In a Healthy Body state, people are generally civil. Like any other circumstance where people share time, space and work, incivility does occur, but when it does, it stands out as uncharacteristic (and undesirable). As demonstrated in the remark above, people feel comfortable calling others on their behavior in a constructive way, while those who originated the behavior tend to own it, and apologize as appropriate. Matters are dealt with, and people move on with increased trust as a result of working through things successfully. Leaders model civility and feel comfortable addressing incivility in constructive and effective ways. Overall, things are well under control, with healthy internal checks and balances that rely on everyone behaving as responsible corporate citizens.

State B: Persistent Allergy

"If he doesn't bother to say hello to me, why should I bother saying hello to him?!"

In a Persistent Allergy state, incivility is quite common, but people don't deal with it or resolve it. Management does not take an active stance to abolish it. In fact, management too is uncivil in many small ways, mostly nonmalicious ways that have to do with personality and habit rather than with intentionally belittling and discounting others. Oftentimes, this state occurs in fast-paced or high-stress environments, where people are busy with important tasks, and task performance takes precedence over relationships.

Despite the fact that no one addresses the incivility, there's a sense of good spirit in these environments, both peer-to-peer and employee-management. The incivility is low intensity rather than high intensity. In essence, if nothing changes, the status quo is tolerable. Much like a nuisance allergy, life goes on, even if at a somewhat less energetic and less healthy pace.

However, allowing this state to persist without sufficient intervention puts the environment at high risk of things developing into a more serious and contaminated state. When this unfolds, you will find yourself in State C or State D—or both.

State C: Chronic Infection

- *"I'm tired of all those whiny callers. They don't pay me enough to deal with this kind of crap."*

- *"You're really asking me to take this thing on? You must be kidding! There's no way I'm doing that, and I don't care if you discipline me for it."*

Chronic Infection is akin to having a full-body inflammation. There is an infestation of incivility across the organization (or unit), and much of it is at high-intensity levels. Malicious and getting-even behaviors are abundant, in both overt and covert ways. Many staff members see themselves as victims of some sort, and justify their own behavior in light of their victimhood. There may be several key instigators, but it is hard to differentiate them from the rest because the work environment is so deeply affected. People have no processes or tools to resolve things peacefully, and any attempt to do so tends to make things worse. Management is unable to address situations effectively, despite trying various strategies to handle specific cases on the ground. However, there's no comprehensive strategy that managers can really use to solve the bigger problems; therefore, resolutions to specific problems are not sustained.

In this state, incivility even pops up in the interface with clients and customers. Staff members (and sometimes managers) refer to customers behind their back in derogatory terms. Uncivil interactions between colleagues occur in front of clients. And, worst of all, clients are sometimes dealt with rudely or indifferently.

In instances of Chronic Infection, the uncivil conduct is directed toward management as well as to other colleagues, as demonstrated in the second quote that opened this section. With lack of organizational support, such as human resources or upper management, managers who are faced with incivility from staff find themselves paralyzed and unable to respond productively.

State D: Acute Disease

"Have you heard about the priest, the rabbi and the imam walking into a bar...?"

"Gosh, it was so funny when we walked into Accounting and saw that fat guy, what's his name? I don't know how he sits in his chair without it breaking. They should make stronger chairs for people from his culture."

Here's where the state of acute disease enters into the picture. When management allows the Persistent Allergy state to endure, over time the uncivil behaviors can easily deteriorate into harassment and even bullying. Jokes that were not funny to begin with turn into full-blown mocking that is based on characteristics such as culture, sexual orientation, gender or race. In some instances, specific people are habitually isolated, ridiculed or marginalized in ways that affect their dignity and may cause them to become sick. Degrading comments—either directed specifically at someone or made in a more general way—create a poisoned work environment.

I refer to these environments as "the Wild West," because lawlessness abounds. Management and human resources have their hands full with harassment complaints, managing sick leaves and the hiring of new people to replace those who have left or are on off work.

IN ALL THE STATES described above, management's role is crucial. You as a leader can shape which path will take hold. If you have felt overwhelmed or if you were at a loss when dealing with similar situations, no worries. As you read further, you will discover the mistakes you should avoid, and specific strategies to guide you step-by-step through many possible scenarios.

INCIVILITY, HARASSMENT AND BULLYING

Workplace incivility is one of many expressions of counterproductive, disrespectful workplace behavior. Closely related to it, and escalating in severity, are harassment and bullying.

Because incivility comprises seemingly insignificant behaviors that are commonplace in every organization, it does not expose your organization (or you as a manager) to notable legal or labor relations risks. Rudeness on your team might damage business, but it will likely not get you into a lawsuit or a labor dispute. Harassment and bullying, on the other hand, are a different matter altogether.

Harassment

The definition of harassment varies from one jurisdiction to the next. Often, as is the case with the United States and Canada, definitions will vary between states and provinces. Generally, harassment refers to unwelcome behavior that demeans, humiliates, intimidates, offends, insults or threatens.

Harassment violates a person's inherent dignity. Harassment can include—but is not limited to—unwelcome sexual behavior, or any comment or display that is based on a person belonging to a certain group, such as of gender, race, ancestry, sexual orientation, age, religion, medical condition, genetic characteristics or disability. In many jurisdictions, human rights legislation deems certain behaviors as harassment because they violate a person's inherent dignity. Nowadays, however, most organizations go well beyond the scope of what is required by legislation and define harassment as encompassing all behaviors that a person knows, or ought reasonably to know, are unwelcome.

Harassment can be intentional and it can be directed at a specific person. However, it can also happen unintentionally. For example, a person can make racist comments stemming from ignorance, or make sexual advances toward someone whom they think is receptive but in fact is far from it. The instigator's intent is not necessarily what determines whether behavior qualifies as harassment or not. Serious weight is given to the fact that the person on the receiving end perceives the behavior as unwelcome. Instead of focusing on the person's intent, many jurisdictions set a standard whereby the person performing the harassment knows, or ought reasonably to have known, that the behavior is unwelcome.

Typically, organizational policies refer to behaviors similar to those listed below as examples of workplace harassment:

- Unwelcome remarks, jokes, innuendos or taunting
- Yelling or shouting that intimidates, coerces, or belittles
- Persistent leering or other obscene or offensive gestures
- Comments, jokes, innuendos, taunting or unwanted actions motivated by or based on a person's belonging to a particular group (such as race, ethnicity, sexual orientation, disability or gender)
- Displaying of electronic or hard-copy information or images that could be offensive, demeaning or derogatory to others (including email, websites and chat rooms)
- Refusal to work or converse with a person or group of persons based on their belonging to a particular group
- Imitation of a person's accent or mannerisms
- Mocking a person's appearance or abilities
- Unwanted and inappropriate physical contact, such as touching, kissing, patting, pinching or brushing up against a person
- Unwelcome sexually oriented remarks, initiations or requests, whether indirect or explicit
- Misuse of authority based on irrelevant factors such as racism, color, age, sex, marital status, sexual orientation or disability

- Offering employment benefits in exchange for a sexual act
- Tampering with a person's personal belongings or work equipment

Harassment does not include appropriate direction, evaluation, appraisal or discipline by a supervisor or manager. However, if you as a manager are not sufficiently thoughtful and cautious, you may find yourself faced with a harassment or even bullying complaint for actions that you have taken in the course of performing your managerial responsibilities (more on this later, in the section on defensive management).

If you allow harassment to take place on your team, you are subjecting yourself and the organization to a range of risks. These include harassment complaints, costly workplace investigations, friction with the union, legal action and claims made to human rights tribunals.

Bullying

Workplace bullying is characterized by its persistent, repetitive nature over time. Unlike harassment, which may in some cases consist of a single event, bullying is a pattern of behavior where one or more persons are mistreated in various negative ways that affect their dignity and destabilize their sense of self or professional standing. The behaviors can be initiated by one person or a group of people. Bullying involves a perceived power imbalance that makes those who are affected by it feel helpless to protect themselves.

Often the bully is a person with hierarchical power within the organization, but that is not always the case. Bullying can also occur between peers and even from an employee toward a manager, who for various reasons feels helpless to self-defend. Bullying tactics can be verbal or nonverbal, psychological, physical, electronic or graphic. And they can be overt or covert, known by many or known by only the target.

Bullying is often associated with behaviors such as those in the list below, repeated regularly over time. As you review the list, you may notice the similarities between some of these behaviors and the ones outlined above as harassment. You might also notice that some of these behaviors are similar to those that we defined as workplace incivility. The key difference (which is part of what makes bullying so harmful to its recipients) is that with bullying the behavior is repeated with some measure of intensity over months or years. The following behaviors, when they occur in clusters and are persistent over time, are typically considered to comprise workplace bullying:

- Put-downs and insults to a person's skills, looks or habits
- Spreading false or malicious rumors, gossip or innuendo
- Berating or belittling an individual
- Repeated, unjust or unwarranted criticism of a person in private or in the presence of others
- Insulting nicknames
- Persistent criticism of one's work
- Practical jokes that humiliate
- Undermining or deliberately impeding a person's work
- Physical gestures that intimidate, offend, degrade or humiliate
- Assigning unreasonable tasks or deadlines to a specific person but not others
- Excessive monitoring of a person's activity
- Excluding or isolating someone from work or social interactions
- "Ganging up" on a person
- Sudden and unpredictable outbursts of anger

- Persistent negative comments in emails, text messages, chat rooms or social media
- Persistently withholding necessary information, or providing the wrong information
- Intruding on a person's privacy by pestering, spying or stalking

It can be difficult to differentiate between incivility, harassment and bullying. After all, we are trying to analyze complex human interactions with numerous variables and package them into predefined categories. For the purposes of this book, the important point for you to consider is that incivility is a key culprit in creating an environment in which harassment and bullying can easily take hold. The more civil the workplace, the less likely it is that harassment and bullying will emerge in the first place, or if they have emerged, that they will be able to persist.

Can Persistent Incivility Amount to Bullying?

Joanna is one of those people who has an annoying voice and can go on and on in tangents. It's really hard to listen to her for more than a few seconds. She's good at her job, but her personal manner has led to team members marginalizing her over time. They take a deep sigh or roll their eyes when she speaks in team meetings, keep her out of the social fabric of things and occasionally enjoy a juicy chat about her annoying ways.

When Joanna asks her manager, Bill, to assist, he informs her that there's nothing that he can really do. "After all," Bill says, "I am a manager, not a social director. Just ignore this nonsense and move on."

Bill's "do nothing" approach is very common. Managers typically perceive this type of dynamic as a mere relationship issue, where the employer has no business or authority to intervene. They observe situations as they unfold right before their eyes without realizing that the matter might get serious. When someone steps forth with a complaint, they don't take meaningful action because they classify the situation as a minor issue in a domain where they should not intervene.

What makes cases like Joanna's so difficult to diagnose (and why so many managers take the wrong action) is that, on the surface, the team's behavior appears to be limited to plain old incivility, with its seemingly insignificant nature. However, the Joannas at the receiving end of these behaviors are likely to experience them as a persistent attack on their dignity and credibility, and they feel unable to protect themselves. They might begin experiencing emotional distress and physical symptoms, to the extent that they may be unable to work. And so, even though no one intends to bully Joanna, the situation as it unfolds looks like a classic bullying situation: one person's dignity and standing are consistently destabilized by others through acts of exclusion and marginalization. As we review some of the research related to social rejection and ostracism later on, you will see how deeply damaging these feelings are, to the extent that the pain can be detected using brain-imaging technology. This case can reasonably be considered bullying, given the persistence of the acts and their far-reaching negative effects on the person.

My recommendation to you is that whenever you become aware of a dynamic where one person is consistency marginalized or ostracized, take it seriously. Do something. These dynamics are your responsibility as the leader, and it is important for you to step up before the situation gets calcified and the affected person gets sick (not to mention unproductive). As the representative of the organization, it is your responsibility—and privilege—to intervene in the social dynamics of a team that persistently ostracizes or scapegoats one of its members.

INVISIBLE CULPRITS: ORGANIZATIONAL CHANGE AND PERSONAL STRESS LEVELS

Throughout my years of consulting and training across sectors, I have observed two key factors that predictably exacerbate workplace incivility.

First, organizational change. When organizations implement change initiatives, stress levels among all those who are affected rise considerably. Starting from the anxiety and worry that precede the change, through the learning curves and confusion that are inherent in its implementation phases, two things happen: First, no one has time for small niceties, and people are more impatient and curt with one another. At the same time, because of the increase of stress-related hormone levels in everyone's bodies and the activation of the body's built-in fight-or-flight stress response, people's sensitivity to incivility that is directed at them intensifies. The reactivity to even minimally rude or insensitive behavior (and the propensity to engage in getting-even activities) also rises. Paradoxically, at the very time when civility would come in most handy, there is deterioration in this arena. As you likely already know from your own experience, these increased incivility problems are bound to impede the success of the change initiative.

The implication for you as a leader is that during times of organizational change, you should take extra care to ensure that civility is maintained. For example, you might initiate team discussions about the issue very early on in the process, or create team norms (sometimes referred to as a team operating agreement or a team charter), where people commit to behaving in a civil fashion throughout the change. Keep this issue firmly in your focus, even as you have so many other things to tend to. Most importantly, make sure to maintain your own civility and to model the desired behaviors yourself.

The second key culprit that affects the degree of civility is each individual's level of personal stress. When people's stress is low, they tend to be more polite, cordial and civil. In this state, when they encounter incivility from another person, they tend to be forgiving, extend the other person the benefit of the doubt and brush the matter off more readily. The opposite is equally true: People who are under the influence of high pressure levels tend to be more short, discourteous and reactive.

Heightened stress levels can emanate from people's work life, but they can stem from other life issues as well, or they can be a combination of both work and home-life pressures. They may have problems at home that contribute to their work stress and vice versa. As the manager, you of course can influence only work-related matters, and should stay away from delving too deeply into the details of people's personal stressors.

Regardless of the source, resilience levels will likely have an impact on civility levels. Therefore, if you wish to boost civility on your team, pay attention to people's stress. Ask yourself what you can do to support resilience and decrease the stressors—and then take action. Equally as important, make sure that your own strain levels are under check, because your own pressure-induced incivility will affect people in ways that you might not realize until much later, if ever. (You will read more about this later, as part of the discussion about the Walk the Talk strategy.)

2

THE EFFECTS OF INCIVILITY ON INDIVIDUALS

....

REAL-LIFE REACTIONS TO WORKPLACE INCIVILITY

It is possible, and easy, to leave workplace incivility alone. After all, why bother trying to tame a phenomenon that is bound to occur wherever you have people operating together as a community of sorts? You can convincingly claim that the ambiguous nature of the behaviors and the even more unclear nature of the intent behind them make it impossible to monitor, measure or abolish incivility. You can persuade yourself and everyone around you that there are more pressing (and important) things to tend to, and why on earth spend precious time and effort on something that is built into any team's DNA?

One answer is that workplace incivility is bad for business. It has measurable, negative effects on individual performance, team performance, customer service, talent retention and employee engagement. From a purely business perspective, civility is not a mere nice-to-have, it is in fact a must-have. While you are busy telling yourself that an abrasive personality cannot be changed, or that gossip is something that cannot be managed, incivility is continuously eroding the fabric of your team and the objectives it is supposed to accomplish. Stay tuned, because in the following section we will explore in depth all the ways in which it impacts a wide range of business indicators.

There's yet another compelling reason for you to bother with workplace incivility and it has more to do with the ethical side of things. A key driver for boosting civility is your obligation to provide those who are in your employ with the conditions that will enable them to perform at their best.

At the heart of any employment contract lies the following commitment: Employees will contribute their time, talent and effort to the employer, and in return the employees will receive a salary, benefits, and safe conditions that will allow them to carry out their job duties to their full potential. As we delve into the actual effects of incivility you will see for yourself why allowing people to be exposed to it without effective intervention by management violates this ethical responsibility. The bottom line is that when incivility reigns, people cannot perform at their best, and you as an employer have failed in keeping your end of this ethical contract.

Furthermore, when you do not actively tame bad behavior on your team, it affects people's perception of you as a leader. You will be viewed as a weak leader who lacks the insight, wisdom and guts to do what's right. Whether it's taking on those "chronic offenders" or addressing head-on problematic interpersonal dynamics, the longer you allow things to fester, the more damage you are doing to your ability to be an effective manager who people want to follow. After all, how can you be an inspiring and trustworthy leader when everyone can see in plain view that you are afraid or unable to do whatever is necessary to create a healthy work environment for all?

So, let's explore the very real business case for stepping up to boost civility. We'll examine the effects of workplace incivility on real people, working in real organizations, under real circumstances. These effects were first uncovered through the pioneering work of Christine Pearson and Christine Porath (along with other collaborators along the way), who published a series of seminal articles on the topic. We'll get to the details of their research a little later in this chapter, but first let's look at the two general responses to incivility.

TEFLON OR VELCRO: THE TWO MAIN REACTIONS TO INCIVILITY

When incivility happens, people respond to it in one of two ways: Teflon or Velcro.

The Teflon approach helps people maintain their equanimity and resilience. And the Velcro approach? Not so much.

Say, for example, that your colleague Marco makes a sarcastic comment to you about your work, in front of a client and another coworker. (This definitely qualifies as incivility.)

With a Teflon approach you essentially let the matter slide right off you, leaving you unaffected by the event. Because you have an excellent relationship with Marco, you may not even notice or register the behavior as problematic to begin with. Or, if you did think of it as inappropriate, you will brush it off by telling yourself that this comment doesn't really matter in the grand scheme of things, or that Marco intended no harm, or that you have more important things to deal with than worry about every little impolite behavior. In other words, with the Teflon approach, you possess a thicker skin to begin with, or you take cognitive action to reframe the situation in ways that help you avoid feeling blame, hurt or a sense of victimization. You simply move on.

To clarify: Teflon doesn't mean that you don't address things with the other person. You certainly might, but because you are not emotionally triggered, you will likely be able to have a conversation with the offender without laying blame or coming across as an angry victim.

A Velcro attitude is an altogether different matter. Here, when an uncivil behavior occurs, you attach yourself to the event both mentally and emotionally, as if you were fastened to it with heavy-duty Velcro.

Here are some of the things you might do when you are in Velcro mode:

- You take it to heart
- You get upset
- You blame and judge the person who was uncivil
- You obsess about it
- You engage in could've-should've thinking
- You are tempted to get even (and often do)
- You vent to others about it
- You carry the upset with you after work hours
- You simply can't shake it off for minutes, hours, days—or longer

In the case of Marco's sarcastic comments in front of a colleague and a client, you could find yourself worrying about what the client and the coworker now think about you; you may feel that Marco has betrayed you and question your friendship; you might begin recalling other little instances that bothered you over the past several years of working together; you'll spend time talking about the event at work or at home; you will get angry at Marco or angry at yourself for having allowed yourself to be so vulnerable; you will feel lonely and anxious... you get the picture.

And if Marco happens to be your boss, your Velcro reaction might be much more intense.

Much of the time, most people are relatively Teflon-ish. After all, there's work to do and things to accomplish, and not every uncivil interaction needs to be taken to heart. But in some instances, Velcro kicks in. And as you already know, none of it is positive or constructive.

MOTIVATION AND ABILITY

- *Stressed from having to deal with two patient emergencies, Dora approaches Cindy to ask for five minutes of her time to help her get some work done so that a patient can get to his MRI test on time. Cindy is clearly enjoying a lull in her work, reading a celebrity magazine. After Dora asks politely for her help, Cindy lifts her eyes and says:*

  "Can't you see I'm busy?! And besides, that's not my job."

- *Bill delivers a report he prepared to Tom, his manager. Tom is relatively new to the role, and Bill spent many hours on the report, thinking that this is his opportunity to impress Tom with his skills. Tom quickly skims over the report and says:*

  "Why didn't you include an executive summary and why on earth are the stats for the last quarter not included? I can't believe you'd submit a report that is so substandard. You should know better."

In the first scenario, the likelihood that Dora will feel upset and insulted is very high. The likelihood that she will be willing to help Cindy if Cindy came to her for help is significantly reduced. Her *motivation* to put in maximum effort is reduced.

In the second scenario, Bill, too, is likely to experience upset and anger. What is added in his case is the element of worry. Back at his desk after this interaction, Bill obsesses over the situation, wondering what exactly his boss meant, why he would do what he did and whether he has now formed a negative opinion of him, which will lead to negative consequences in the long term. For the next couple of hours he finds it difficult to focus. He goes for a longer-than-usual lunch break. He gets on the phone with his wife, seeking her support and advice. Moving from the stinging pain, now Bill tries to assess the situation in what researchers[4] refer to as the Appraisal Phase: He is trying to regain control and balance by assessing all aspects of the situation and trying to put it into perspective. Meanwhile, his *ability* to do his job is temporarily compromised.

Christine Pearson and Christine Porath's research demonstrates that people's reactions to incivility fall under two overarching categories: motivation and ability.[5] As illustrated in the two scenarios above, their research suggests that when people are treated in an uncivil manner, they stop performing as well as they should, either because they are no longer motivated to do so, or because they are in some way compromised and, therefore, are unable to do so.

WHAT THE RESEARCH TELLS US

Pearson and Porath uncovered numerous grim effects that incivility exacts on individuals, including the following.[6]

Among workers who have been on the receiving end of incivility, here's how *motivation* was affected:

- 48% intentionally decrease their work effort
- 47% intentionally decreased the time spent at work
- 38% intentionally decreased the quality of their work

Here's the story that these numbers tell: Almost one out of two people will purposely lower their work effort and the time they spend at work. They might do this for a few minutes, hours or days, or maybe even for months or years. They might take longer breaks, take a sick day or go home rather than put in extra time. They might deliver sloppy work, or omit details that are crucial to excellent results. They might slow their work down.

And here's how *ability* was affected:

- 80% lost time worrying
- 63% lost time avoiding the offender
- 66% said that their performance declined

Christine Porath and collaborator Amir Erez set out to examine more specifically what happens to a person's ability to perform after being exposed to incivility.[7] Their work shows that being exposed to even a single event of rudeness is harmful to task performance, focus, helpfulness and creativity.

One of the fascinating aspects their findings highlight is that subjects who merely imagined that they were treated uncivilly (they were given scenarios describing rude behavior and asked to imagine it happened to them) performed more poorly on routine and creative tasks than when not exposed to rudeness.

I must confess that, at first, Pearson and Porath's far-reaching results seemed unfathomable to me and, in fact, exaggerated. It was also hard to tell whether the intense reactions that they were describing applied across the board, or were more exclusive to situations where the instigators were habitual offenders, or possibly people with more hierarchical power.

So I decided to collect my own data, using two constituencies to which I had easy access. The first group was Bar-David Consulting's workshop audiences. The second was human resource professionals across Canada with whom I was connected through my ongoing role as a contributor to *Canadian HR Reporter*, Canada's leading human resources publication.

I began polling participants in my training sessions about their perceptions of the effects of incivility. I asked them (and in fact continue to do so) to rely on their own observations and wisdom to guess what Pearson and Porath had discovered in their research. For example, I might pick one of the research findings and ask my audience, "What percentage of people reported that they purposely lowered their work effort in response to incivility?"

By and large, the real-life observations of these participants (who represent all industries, at all organizational levels) are similar to those found by researchers. Furthermore, when I ask the questions without providing a multiple-choice option, their guesses are even higher than the numbers the existing research has uncovered.

Concurrently, I partnered with *Canadian HR Reporter* in 2011 to conduct a survey that would garner comprehensive information about the effects of incivility on the Canadian workplace. Over three hundred professionals representing a wide range of industries[8] responded with compelling information about the impact of incivility on individuals, teams and organizations.[9] Their observations, which you will hear about throughout this chapter, confirm the kind of impact that Pearson and Porath identified in their research. In fact, here too, in many cases the figures that our respondents came up with were even higher than those of the researchers.

So, not only did my own research confirm Pearson's and Porath's rigorous study of incivility in the workplace, but I was surprised by the intensity of the data I was collecting on the ground.

Clearly, incivility has a profound effect on human beings. The impact of each event might last minutes, hours, days or even years, and it all adds up. It is challenging to arrive at an exact monetary estimate of the costs triggered by workplace incivility. Still, the Implementation Clinic titled "The Dollars and Cents" in chapter 3 will introduce you to a simple way of conducting a monetary analysis and will guide you in how you can execute your own calculation—even if only in general terms.

The bottom line is that people who are upset, distracted or worried because of incivility cannot perform at their best. The worry and anxiety are not only disruptive and demotivating; they also make them more prone to illness, and the reduction in task performance makes them more likely to have accidents and make mistakes on the job. Over time, if exposure to incivility is repeated and frequent, a person is disposed to develop anxiety disorders and even depression. Such exposure will exacerbate preexisting mental and physical symptoms.

In Canada, a cross-country initiative is attempting to address this matter. In January 2013, the Mental Health Commission of Canada launched the National Standard of Canada on Psychological Health and Safety in the Workplace. The Commission (established by the Canadian government to serve as a catalyst for promoting better mental health and changing Canadians' attitudes toward mental health) developed the standard in response to growing awareness that compromised workplace conditions can trigger or exacerbate mental illness, and to the corresponding recognition that employers have a duty to provide an environment that supports mental health. The standard outlines a systematic approach to developing and sustaining a psychologically healthy and safe workplace. It lists thirteen factors that affect psychological health in the workplace. One of them is *civility and respect*, which is defined as follows on the Mental Health Commission of Canada's website, where the full standard can be found:

> Civility and respect is present in a work environment where workers are respectful and considerate in their interactions with one another, as well as with customers, clients, and the public. Civility and respect are based on showing esteem, care, and consideration for others, and acknowledging their dignity.

The standard is a voluntary tool and the results will not be known for a while. Some progressive employers have already begun to implement its tools and processes. One can expect that over time many others will follow.

GUERILLA WARFARE ON THE JOB, OR THE SPIRAL EFFECT

- *"I used to say good morning to her, but I stopped. If she doesn't bother acknowledging my presence when I'm three steps away, then why should I say good morning to her?!"*

- *"I don't need those kinds of sarcastic comments from a manager. That's rude. His mother should have done a better job raising him. I make sure to warn other people about the kind of person that he is."*

- *"She's always late to meetings. So sometimes I give her a taste of her own medicine and arrive a few minutes late when I have to relieve her from shift. It's quite amusing to see her running to catch her bus on time."*

These examples highlight common dynamics that you have seen (and maybe even been part of) numerous times. People use getting-even tactics to respond to what they perceive as mini-aggression directed at them. They may not think of them as "tactics"; however, these actions are akin to moves on a chessboard: one player makes a move, and the other player makes a countermove.

First described by Andersson and Pearson,[10] the spiral effect begins with one or more persons engaging in uncivil behavior that upsets another person, and continues in a chain of downward-spiraling events where each party ups the ante. These actions are intended to balance the imaginary ledger of justice. When people are upset by someone's incivility, they react in proportion to the perceived seriousness of the offense. A common example is the "She does not say hello." When Luanne does not respond to Emma's simple hello, Emma will react by ceasing to say hello to Luanne—a punishment that she perceives as proportionate to the offense. But over time, if Luanne continues to falter in the hello department, Emma will add additional getting-even tactics to the original one; she might throw a bit of gossip into the mix, or an occasional work-related sabotage. In other words, a chronic offense is deemed to require an elevated getting-even response to satisfy the person who perceives himself or herself as the victim. This elevated retaliatory response gives the original victim of the incivility the sense that those invisible ledgers of justice are adequately balanced. (In fact, there is a body of research that shows that people resort to various forms of sabotage and even theft in an attempt to restore justice after being treated unfairly.) However, sadly, all this eye-for-an-eye behavior does is drag both parties down into an endless negative spiral of incivility.

Here are some common getting-even strategies:[11]

1. Repeating the same behavior that the first person performed

2. Giving the "silent treatment"

3. "Forgetting" something when someone needs it

4. Broadcasting the news about the person's behavior, and other forms of gossip

5. Ignoring or responding slowly to requests

6. Sabotaging the other person or the work itself

7. "Working to rule," putting in only the minimum effort and time necessary

As identified by Andersson and Pearson, on some occasions these spiraling mini-aggression activities can reach a tipping point, after which the nature of the behaviors becomes more serious. Mini-aggression incivility gets replaced with blatant aggression and destructive actions, possibly even violence. This is where your role as a leader is crucial; early diagnosis on your part and thoughtful intervention will prevent things from becoming more serious. Mind the Windows, one of the strategies you will find later on in the book, will help you develop a better understanding about your role in such matters.

IMPLEMENTATION CLINIC

Effects on Individuals:
The Complex World of Emotions

When a person takes an incivility incident to heart (the Velcro reaction), he or she will experience a potent cocktail of emotions.

EXERCISE:
Consider a situation where you personally were affected by incivility. Next, refer to the list of emotions that appears on the following pages and circle all the words that apply to your reaction at that time.

As you reflect on the words that you have circled...

- What do you discover or rediscover about yourself?

- How do these insights impact your perceptions of other people's reactions to incivility?

- What is one action you can take based on your answers to the above two questions?

How will you use the emotions list to help boost civility on your team?

* * *

Disillusioned	Disrespectful	Gloomy
Distrustful	Ticked off	Disheartened
Misgiving	Revengeful	Down
Lost	Reactive	Despondent
Unsure	Venomous	Stuck
Uneasy	Irate	Contracted
Irritated	Short-tempered	Tight
Hostile	Stubborn	Blocked
Annoyed	Nervous	Despairing
Upset	Scared	Hopeless
Hateful	Worried	Dismayed
Aggressive	Rebellious	Oversensitive
Bitter	Exasperated	Remorseful
Frustrated	Impatient	Grouchy
Resentful	Contrary	"Off"
Malicious	Condemning	Moody
Infuriated	Seething	Crabby
Critical	Disappointed	Morose
Mean-spirited	Discouraged	Cranky
Vindictive	Ashamed	Grumpy
Mean	Powerless	Burdened
Spiteful	Diminished	Negative
Furious	Miserable	Closed
Agitated	Self-denigrating	Out of sorts
Antagonistic	Self-hating	No energy
Mad	Sulky	Shaky
Incensed	Low	Touchy
Scornful	Lousy	Drawn
Sarcastic	Alienated	Doubtful
Sharp	Pessimistic	Uncertain
Poisonous	Dejected	Perplexed
Insulted	Self-critical	Embarrassed

Hesitant	Inept	Apprehensive
Tense	Incapacitated	Aggressive
Stressed	Shut down	Defensive
Uncomfortable	Cut off	Enraged
Superior	Trapped	Fearful
Disdainful	Weak	Suspicious
Manipulative	Sick	Anxious
Judgmental	Nauseated	Alarmed
Prejudiced	Fidgety	Panicked
Argumentative	Trembling	Frightened
Condescending	Squirming	Guarded
Demanding	Jittery	Troubled
Confounded	Woozy	Self-absorbed
Distracted	Twitching	Rigid
Disoriented	Weary	Phobic
Off-kilter	Preoccupied	Intolerant
Frenzied	Cold	Disturbed
Awkward	Lifeless	Disrupted
Incapable	Uncaring	Intimidated
Alone	Uninterested	Avoiding
Paralyzed	Unresponsive	Unwelcoming
Fatigued	Tired	Unbending
Useless	Robotic	Paranoid
Inferior	Slow	Inhibited
Vulnerable	Sluggish	Immobile
Empty	Shaky	Prejudiced
Distressed	Restless	Self-conscious
Pathetic	Threatened	Crushed
Distraught	Cowardly	Tormented
Doomed	Insecure	Deprived
Overwhelmed	Wary	Pained
Incompetent	Uptight	Tortured

Rejected	Bullied	Discontented
Offended	Slighted	Crying
Afflicted	Belittled	Stony
Aching	Tearful	Serious
Victimized	Sorrowful	Stern
Heartbroken	Anguished	Frowning
Agonized	Desolate	Recoiling
Appalled	Unhappy	Glaring
Wronged	Lonely	Disgusted
Humiliated	Grieved	Attacked
Upset	Mournful	Attacking
Insulted	Sullen	Tactless
Withdrawn	Sour	Hurtful
Miffed	Injured	Stilted
Indignant	Unworthy	Stiff
Suffering	Fragile	Combative
Distant	Disconnected	Complaining
Invaded	Devastated	Obsessive
Bulldozed	Blindsided	Blunt

*Note: This list is based on similar lists in the public domain, widely used in the personal growth movement for several decades.

3

HOW INCIVILITY AFFECTS TEAMS, ORGANIZATIONAL INDICATORS AND CUSTOMER SERVICE

Three children sliding on the ice
upon a summer's day,
As it fell out, they all fell in,
The rest they ran away.
—Mother Goose, "Three Children on the Ice"

The impact that incivility has on individuals is only the beginning of the story. Individual responses translate into the ways that people approach their work, their time, each other, the customers they serve, their commitment to the organization, and their willingness to go the extra mile (or not). Any change in any of these variables has ramifications on your business and brand. Incivility that goes unchecked can spread like wildfire through your organization and business culture as it proliferates. We will travel through several spheres together over the following pages: We will look at the effects that incivility has on teams and on customer service, innovation, retention, commitment and engagement. Finally, we will take a peek behind the scenes as we look at some of the underlying forces that lead people to respond in such powerful ways to workplace incivility.

TEAM EFFECTS

Once individuals are affected by workplace incivility, the negative impact on a team's dynamics and performance is inevitable.

No one thrives on a team where people are rude to each other, dismiss each other's work, skip greetings or roll eyes, gossip or use sarcasm. In such environments, the word "team" turns into an empty shell. Below is a list of typical damage that incivility inflicts on a team:

- **Purpose and goals.** The team's purpose and goals suffer when incivility is present. Take for example a surgical unit in a hospital, where the goal is to provide patients with the best care possible before and after surgery. When the nurses argue loudly in the nursing station, it does not contribute to good care. An upset nurse can give a patient the wrong medication, or lash out at cleaning staff who will then be unable to clean properly, leading to potentially dangerous contamination. And when a nurse takes a longer break in the washroom after having received a dressing-down from a colleague in front of others, the woman in labour at the end of the hallway is delayed in receiving the assistance that she desperately needs. As such, the team is failing daily in living up to its very reason for being.

- **Help and support.** People who experience incivility are not motivated to help each other. When incivility sets into the team's culture, people get more protective of their territory and less inclined to look out for others or help one another.

    In an interesting part of their research,[12] Porath and Erez found that subjects were significantly less likely to show helpful behaviors toward the person whom they perceived to be rude; in addition, they were less likely to be helpful even when the person they were helping was not the rude person nor seemed to be connected to the rude person. When an experimenter knocked a jar with ten pens off a desk, those who were exposed to uncivil behavior earlier helped pick up only two pens on average. However, those participants who were not exposed to rude behavior picked up close to eight pens on average.

- **Factions.** Some incivility situations lead to the creations of factions and camps within the team. The fractures can happen across cultural lines, such as when one group of people speaks a second language in ways that make others feel excluded and marginalized. Other times the lines are drawn (often unintentionally) by a group of people who enjoy close ties based on things such as professional designation or having been part of another organization that amalgamated into the current organization. These people create an invisible yet impenetrable exclusionary line around themselves.

- **Communication.** Team communication is also profoundly affected by workplace incivility. When members are uncivil to one another, they stop communicating directly, or their communication with each other becomes stifled and ineffective. You may well have seen situations where one team member is not speaking to another and work-related communication becomes problematic. And when the Spiral Effect is present, team members sometimes purposely refrain from providing their colleagues with information that is crucial to them carrying out their job duties successfully.

- **Work processes.** Work processes become skewed and ineffective over time when incivility is in the mix. Say for example that the proper flow of work requires that Sergio forward data to Jenna, who works on it before transferring it to Soheila, from whom it goes to Frank, who puts all the data together and sends it along to another department. But there's one little problem: Soheila is chronically sarcastic and moody and one never knows what mood she will be in on any given day. After several months of going through trials and tribulations trying to deal with Soheila's uncivil treatment every time she has to hand work over to her, Jenna is worn down. She can't stand the thought of dealing with moody Soheila anymore. She decides she needs help and, because she happens to have a really good relationship with Sergio, she turns to him to help her deal with Soheila. Jenna pleads with Sergio over a series of discussions to agree to a little workaround that will enable her to avoid dealing with Soheila (these discussions of course take lots of time, in which no work is being performed).

Under Jenna's proposed workaround, instead of handing the work to Soheila as she is supposed to do, Jenna will instead give her completed work back to Sergio, who will in turn submit it to Soheila. Finally Sergio agrees. Several months pass and Sergio, too, is worn down from his dealings with Soheila. He tells Jenna he can no longer deal with Soheila and she needs to find another solution. Jenna, in her anxiety at the prospect of having to resume direct contact with Soheila, now turns to Frank and asks that he help her… and so this goes on, with time wasted and inefficiencies created. Finally the manager (who, frankly, was asleep at the helm) hears about all this and decides that the workflow needs to be redesigned, given that everyone finds it impossible to work with Soheila. Now the manager devises new workarounds to "deal with" the problem. None of this makes sense from a business perspective, nor a team performance perspective, but that is what incivility can do.

CUSTOMER SERVICE

I once received a voicemail message from a woman who identified herself as Christina, a human resources director in a construction company. She stated that she would like to discuss the possibility of Bar-David Consulting offering training within her organization. She did not specify what type of training they were seeking, and since our firm offers various types of training and consulting services, I was looking forward to hearing from her about their needs and discussing what programs might be best suited to meet those needs.

When I called back, a receptionist answered the line with a curt, unfriendly tone, announcing the company name. I asked for Christina. The next thing I knew, without further ado, I heard the ringing tone of Christina's line. The receptionist had not bothered with any cordial response, such as "I'll transfer you right now," or "Please hold the line" or even a simple "One moment, please."

This lack of basic courtesy, combined with her curt tone, led me to believe what proved to be right: the company was seeking training focused on workplace incivility.

If you think that incivility on your team will not affect the interface with customers, clients and patients, I suggest you think again. Invariably, one of the following is bound to happen (a partial list):

- A client will witness your staff's incivility, and will make decisions based on their impressions.
- A staff member who is used to treating colleagues discourteously will inadvertently deal with a customer the same way.
- Team members who are used to being dismissive with each other will refer to clients behind their back in derogatory ways, possibly attaching unflattering nicknames to them.
- The derogatory nicknames that are used to refer to clients spill into "prohibited grounds," where clients are referred to in terms that are based on their culture, religion or race.

- Your staff is distracted by colleagues' incivility. They make mistakes, take longer breaks, forget information, spread gloom rather than cheeriness, and offer no creative solutions when those are needed. Customers naturally conclude that your organization offers inferior service and products.

The data from my survey for *Canadian HR Reporter* revealed that these effects are nothing to sneeze at.[13] As many as 72 percent of our respondents "strongly agreed" or "somewhat agreed" that incivility has a significant negative effect on customer service. This number is even more significant when you consider that human resource professionals (who were the respondents in this survey) do not always have the opportunity to observe interactions with customers as they occur and might, therefore, not be as acutely aware of all the small and not-so-small ways that incivility erodes the company-client relationship, and along with it the company brand.

Furthermore, in Bar-David Consulting's training sessions, when we ask participants (again, in a wide range of industries) to guess what percent of people take their frustration out on customers after they experience incivility on the job, the vast majority come up with figures that range between 60 and 80 percent. These figures are much higher than those reported by Pearson and Porath, who found that 25 percent of people they studied admitted to taking their frustrations out on a customer.[14] When we ask our participants why they offer such high estimates, the response is that people who take their frustration out on a customer are often unaware that they are doing so. For example, they are upset about something that happened in the backroom with a colleague, and when they deal with a customer immediately afterward they are not consciously aware of the fact that they are coming across as short, upset or anxious. While the employee may not know that he or she is affected in these ways, it is safe to assume that the customer certainly does.

IMPACT ON INNOVATION

If your organization or team relies on innovation for its success, then you have a vested interest in ensuring that civility levels on your team are high. When people feel that their ideas might be belittled or that their input will be rudely dismissed, they become risk-averse. They shift into survival-and-safety mode. In this mode, creative problem solving is inhibited and conformity reigns. Innovation, which relies on taking risks, is stifled.

The research by Porath and Amir Erez[15] demonstrates that study participants who were exposed to rudeness from a person of authority or from a peer performed more poorly on creativity tasks than did those who were treated in a civil fashion. For example, they report that participants who had been treated badly and then asked what to do with a brick proposed solid yet uncreative ideas such as "build a house," "build a wall" and "build a school." On the other hand, participants who were dealt with in a civil manner and then asked the same question came up with much more imaginative ideas for things to do with a good old brick. Their suggestions included "sell the brick on eBay," "use it as a goalpost for a street soccer game," "hang it on a museum wall and call it abstract art," and "decorate it like a pet and give it to a kid as a present."[16]

Civility means that everyone's expertise and contribution are respected. Innovation thrives in a fear-free environment.

RETENTION, COMMITMENT, ENGAGEMENT

I once gave a workshop to a group of leaders from a variety of organizations. When I raised the topic of the interplay between incivility and retention of talent, one participant chimed in with the following story:

The organization he worked for was searching for someone to fill a director's position. One of the candidates stood out as particularly suited for the job—a perfect fit. During the first interview this person was enthusiastic about the prospect of working for the organization. During the second interview the candidate seemed more cautious about the job. Still, he was the perfect fit and he was offered the job. Surprisingly, he declined.

It took much probing until he shared what led to his decision: "When I came for the first interview and met my interviewers, I thought I had found my dream job. The role was fantastic and the organizational values resonated deeply with my own belief system. But when I sat in the reception area waiting for my second interview, I happened to observe a rude exchange between the receptionist and one of the staff members, with a manager overlooking the exchange and doing nothing. This gave me a totally different perspective about the organization and made me realize that there was a big gap between the organization's stated values and the way those values are lived on the ground. I decided that this was not a good choice for me."

Workplace incivility, especially when it is pervasive, exacts a price well beyond its effects on individuals, teams, customer service and even innovation. It also affects engagement, commitment to the organization, retention and attraction of talent.

In Pearson and Porath's research, 78 percent of participants reported that their commitment to the organization declined, and 12 percent said that they left their job because of the uncivil treatment.[17] Essentially, four out of five employees were less committed because of incivility, and one out of eight went as far as leaving their employer because of workplace incivility issues. These are critical losses that often go unnoticed.

The survey that I conducted with *Canadian HR Reporter* offers interesting further food for thought. Table 2 shows the percentage of survey respondents who "strongly agreed" or "somewhat agreed" that incivility had a significant negative effect on key organizational indicators such as productivity, inter-team collaboration and customer service. As you will readily see, the impact was highly significant.

Table 2: *Canadian HR Reporter* **Survey: Negative Impact of Incivility on Key Organizational Indicators**[18]

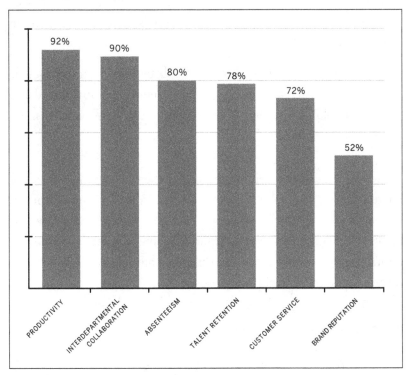

These figures are striking, even shocking. They tell us that incivility poses a tangible risk to organizations. When you compound the effects of incivility on individuals, as outlined earlier, with the effects on teams, innovation and customer service, what you get is a hefty price tag that goes well beyond monetary value. When your brand is eroding, customers are going elsewhere, you're having difficulty attracting and retaining talent and the cost of sick leaves is rising, your capacity to carry out the organization's objectives is severely hampered.

WHY SUCH EXTREME RESPONSES TO INCIVILITY?

When you sit back and consider the facts and figures noted above, a few questions emerge:

- Why on earth would adults respond in such extreme ways to seemingly insignificant rude behaviors, when it is not even clear that the person had any intent to harm?
- Why aren't people more Teflon-like, shrugging off or even laughing at an instance of incivility, and then moving on, unaffected and without holding a grudge? Why do they, in such large numbers, Velcro themselves onto the situation?

To understand why humans respond in the ways that they do, allow me to take you on a behind-the-scenes tour. Much like the computers that serve us, we humans possess "operating systems" that define our predictable responses to certain stimuli. Specifically, let's examine two built-in survival systems that exist in every human: the fight-or-flight response, and the ostracism-detection system.

The Fight-or-Flight Response

The fight-or-flight response is a natural reaction to danger in both humans and animals. It is a built-in response that triggers physiological changes to give the body the strength necessary to flee a threatening situation or to fight the danger it encounters. Faced with an imminent threat, unnecessary functions shut down and vital functions that are necessary for dealing with the threat are enhanced. Hormones such as adrenaline and cortisol (also known as the stress hormone) are released. There are increases to heart rate, blood pressure and muscle tension, as well as many more physiological changes that place the body on high alert. When the fight-or-flight response is triggered, the part of the brain called the amygdala gets activated as well. In what Daniel Goleman coined "an amygdala hijack," this little part of the brain, in charge of emotions, bypasses the rational brain. Rather than acting from the rational part of the brain, a person's actions are directed by the emotional, primitive part, where the responses to threats are irrational and even destructive.

You may be wondering what this has to do with people's responses to workplace incivility. Well…

As early as 135 A.C.E., the Greco-Roman philosopher Epictetus had written, "Man is disturbed not by things, but by the views he takes of them." Indeed, the way we think about a situation, regardless of whether or not our thinking is accurate, can switch on the fight-or-flight response. Our bodies can't tell the difference between the thought "An eighteen-wheel truck is heading right toward me at seventy-five miles per hour!" and the thought "Wendy just made a fool of me in front of everybody." Any stress, whether physical, psychological or emotional, will produce elements of the fight-or-flight response and the associated hijack.

Here's how it plays out when incivility happens: John rolls his eyes in the middle of Neil's presentation. Neil's fight-or-flight response engages, causing him to experience raw emotions, characterized by black and white thinking, with no shades of gray. And when Suzie makes a disparaging comment to Francine in front of a patient and his family, Francine's years of training as a nurse and pride in her professional demeanor may not necessarily come to her aid in that moment because her brain is now running on its survival operating system rather than on its thoughtful, emotionally intelligent one.

In cases of incivility, the fight-or-flight response is at the heart of many of the disproportionate reactions to seemingly insignificant discourteous behavior. This is a key reason people react in the ways that we have described earlier in this chapter: They purposely lower their work effort and the time they spend at work, they engage in retaliatory acts and they lose significant time worrying and obsessing over incivility incidents they experience.

The potent fight-or-flight hormonal cocktail also affects concentration and judgment, which in turn can have an effect on both safety and performance. In this state, Francine is more likely to give the patient the wrong medication, and Neil, driving his forklift after his presentation, might inadvertently get into an accident.

Incivility and Ostracism

Consider this: What is the common denominator between—

- a teacher removing a child from her peers,
- a religious institution excommunicating a deviant member, and
- a husband giving his wife the "silent treatment"?

Answer: All three are ostracism practices that have withstood the test of time, across cultures and religions. They have survived because exclusion is an unbearable threat. Our species is hardwired to respond acutely to any sign of social rejection because, from the beginning of time, any sign of elimination by the tribe carried the threat of being physically banished from the community and left to fend for ourselves in harsh circumstances and ultimately perish. From an evolutionary perspective, the equation is brutally simple: If you're not one of the tribe, you die.

With this in mind, Dr. Kipling Williams and other researchers in the ostracism field speculated that humans are, therefore, equipped with extremely sensitive sensors for detecting even the most remote signal of potential removal from the tribe. They set up fun experiments where, for example, an unsuspecting subject walks into an elevator and either gets acknowledged by those already riding in it or is ignored by them. Their research consistently finds that even short exposures to rejection experiences create a reflexive increase in anger and sadness and lower people's levels of meaningful existence, belonging and self-esteem.[19] Not surprisingly, they find that the intensity of the ostracism experience is directly related to the intensity and duration of the reaction: Longer and more serious rejection experiences will trigger stronger and more lasting reactions.

In a series of cyberball-tossing experiments for which he became known, Dr. Williams and his colleagues placed a subject under an fMRI and asked him or her to play a game of virtual toss-ball with two other people, who were represented by cute little animated figures. (An fMRI is a medical imaging machine that enables researchers to measure brain activity in real time.) The ball is tossed to the study subject once or twice near the beginning of the game, and then the game continues for an additional thirty to fifty throws in which the participant never receives the ball. They found that the subject's dorsal anterior cingulate cortex fired up, exactly as it would have flared up had someone smashed the person's finger with a hammer.[20] Indeed, this research shows that our brain's pain center gets fired up because of a perfectly inconsequential game, played for less than three minutes, with imaginary people you can't see and will never meet.

The research on social rejection offers an interesting explanation as to why people respond to incivility in the many, and sometimes extreme, ways described earlier in this chapter. If insignificant interactions with total strangers affect mood, self-esteem and even the pain center in the brain, it is no wonder that two out of three people will report to researchers that the quality of their work deteriorated after an incivility occurrence, or that four out of five will report that they lost time worrying after an incident.

IMPLEMENTATION CLINIC

The Dollars and Cents

You can get a sense of the monetary cost of workplace incivility quite readily by nailing down basic figures.

Below you will find a generic template that you can adapt to fit your own circumstances.

As you insert figures into the relevant spots, stick to conservative estimates. Doing so will help you feel confident that your final results are reliable.

The calculation includes the toll that incivility exacts only at the *affected person's* level. It does *not* include other organizational costs or expenditures, such as lost management or human resources time, costs of mediation or investigations, grievances, departures from the organization, hiring and training costs, loss of customers or other related expenses. You can add these at your own discretion.

THE PROCESS

Step 1
Ask yourself: How many times a week does an average employee in your organization experience an incivility incident that he or she Velcros onto? (See page 35 for a detailed discussion of Velcro- and Teflon-like reactions to incivility.) That is, the incident upsets or distracts the person, even in a relatively minor fashion. (Select a conservative figure.)

Step 2
Examine the categories listed in the calculation sample on page 64 and enter conservative figures for each, based on your familiarity with your particular organizational culture. For example, if people in your

organization tend to vent to a colleague about upsetting events, you might enter fifteen minutes for person A (the speaker), and twenty minutes for person B (the listener). If in your organization people do less of that, then enter only five minutes for each, or none at all.

Step 3
Add additional categories as you see fit. For example, if people in your organization tend to take sick time whenever they are upset, add a sick-time category.

Remember that the calculations suggested here are partial and conservative. They do not include other costs beyond the effects on individuals.

* * *

IMPLEMENTATION CLINIC

Sample Calculation

Let's assume you work for an organization of 500 employees, with an average hourly salary rate of $35 per hour.

	Example	Your Figures
Average number of Velcro events per employee per week	1 per week	_____
Time lost in worry and preoccupation about the event	10 minutes	_____
Purposely lowering work effort	5 minutes	_____
Purposely decreasing time spent on work (leaving early, longer breaks, not working overtime)	5 minutes	_____
Time lost speaking about the situation with a colleague	5 minutes	_____
Colleague's time lost in above conversation	5 minutes	_____
Total time per week	**30 minutes**	_____

Cost incurred in above example:

30 minutes per week x 50 weeks per year = 25 hours a year

Cost per employee: 25 hours x $35 hourly pay = $875 per year

Total cost to the organization: $875 x 500 employees = $437,500

4

WHY INCIVILITY PERSISTS DESPITE THE DAMAGE IT CREATES

By this point you might be asking yourself: If workplace incivility leaves such havoc in its wake, why on earth does it continue to thrive? What factors enable and support it?

You probably already have your own answers to this question, rooted in your experiences and observations. Your career path would have provided you with ample opportunities to encounter a wide range of circumstances, each with its own dynamics of triggers and enabling factors. You may have already concluded that incivility persists as a result of interplay between various factors, some or all of which form a part in the seven top organization-based reasons why incivility persists:

1. Not connecting the dots
2. Nonexistent or weak organizational values
3. Ineffective organizational processes and solutions
4. Uncivil organizational culture
5. Management-union issues
6. Incivility at the top
7. Leaders' omissions, mistakes and oversights

Let's examine these one by one.

NOT CONNECTING THE DOTS

There is a glaring incongruence between the magnitude of the incivility risk and organizational responses to it. This disconnect stems from organizational decision makers' lack of appreciation of the far-reaching impact of incivility and the costs that it exacts. This phenomenon is evidenced in the responses we got to our *Canadian HR Reporter* study described earlier, where the majority of respondents (81 percent) stated that they "wish management was more aware of how incivility impacts the business," and a whopping 72 percent stated that they "wish they had more organizational support" to address things.[21] When management, especially senior management, does not see the impact, the natural consequence is a lack of support for human resources or for managers on the ground to address these issues.

To begin with, most organizations are unfamiliar with the label "workplace incivility." When you don't have a term that will accurately capture the problem, you are likely to take the wrong action, or take no action at all. The ambiguous nature of workplace incivility and the seemingly intangible nature of its impact make it an invisible disease that, therefore, seems to have no discernible effect.

Let's look at another disease, such as bulimia (known formally as bulimia nervosa). Until Gerald Russell first published a description of the symptoms and manifestations of this illness in 1979, people across the world who experienced a morbid fear of getting fat were suffering from the effects of overeating-purging, but were not getting the help they desperately needed. Their families and medical supports did not have a label for what these (mostly) women were experiencing, nor well-defined strategies to help alleviate their suffering. I clearly recall a teenaged friend of mine who used to purge regularly and encouraged the rest of us to do so too (I was physically unable to, but I sure tried a few times). It never dawned on me that this was actually a disease with serious ramifications, and, therefore, I never suggested that she seek help. After bulimia was added to the DSM-III (the "bible" of psychiatric diagnostics), there was a massive swelling of documented incidences of the disease. Once the medical community, families and society had a name for the phenomenon, everyone started connecting the dots. Families and friends became alert to the problem, and specialized treatments were offered.

Similarly, as long as organizations don't make the connections between workplace incivility and business indicators such as talent retention, absenteeism, and low productivity, incivility will endure as a nameless disease—unnoticed and, therefore, untended. Through my training and consulting experience I learned that once we introduce our clients to the concept of incivility, they are able to diagnose it properly and then take effective action, in the exact same way that the medical community awoke to the existence of the disease called bulimia. Simply identifying and naming this organizational malady can go a long way.

WEAK OR NONEXISTENT ORGANIZATIONAL VALUES

In a leadership development session I facilitated in the not-for-profit sector, I asked a question that I often ask: "So, what are your organization's values?" The sixteen attendees scrambled as they tried to retrieve the answers from somewhere in the labyrinth of their memories, unsuccessfully.

The executive director chimed in with "Wait a second, I should know this! We just created new values a few months ago, together with the board!" She burst out laughing, admitting that it was embarrassing that even she herself did not know what the values were.

(By the way, do you know your organizational values off the top of your head?)

The purpose of organizational values is to offer a set of principles that people can rely on to guide decisions on an ongoing basis; they create a shared language that shapes the culture. A value of "excellence," for example, will inform a wide range of decisions, such as who gets promoted, which products are sold, or whether or not to extend the life of a project to ensure a superior result.

When organizational values are weak or nonexistent, things are ambiguous and it is more difficult for a manager to take a firm stand on incivility, especially if other managers are not taking the same stance. Conversely, when the value of "respect" (or related values such as integrity, honesty, community, accountability or trust) is included in the formal organizational values, it increases the chances that incivility will be dealt with effectively. In such cases, clear responsibilities and accountabilities can be articulated and maintained. There is a standard against which actions and decisions can be held. For example, a manager can easily address a situation by saying something as simple as "Jokes of this nature do not align with our company's commitment to respect and integrity. Let's cut it out."

My work has taught me that it is surprisingly common for leaders (and, even more so, staff) to be unfamiliar with the stated organizational values. In some organizations the formal values may not necessarily be known, but people across the board still do have a strong sense of the company's underlying fundamental values, and they guide their decisions based on these principles. However, such informal commitment to the values risks leaving your corporate standards ambiguous, and robs you as a leader of the ability to leverage the values to assist you in achieving top-notch results through and with your people. The same holds true when the organization does have a set of formal values but they serve as nice wall decoration without anyone truly knowing and owning them. In these cases, too, leaders are unable to use the values to everyone's benefit.

As a manager, you can build the organization's values into everything you do. Examples include spending time reviewing them with any person who joins the team, relaying the role that the values played in decisions you have made, referring to them frequently in your verbal or written communication and encouraging team members to use the values lens to guide the interactions within the team and with outsiders.

INEFFECTIVE ORGANIZATIONAL PROCESSES AND SOLUTIONS

In many organizations, incivility persists simply because it can. Insufficient organizational processes and a lack of effective tools for early detection and preventive action contribute to this result. And when action is taken, it is often not the right one. In short, organizations don't create the right infrastructure to begin with, and when they are called to respond, they throw the wrong solutions at the problem.

Some organizations lack foundational documents such as a respectful workplace policy or a code of conduct. In other workplaces, these documents exist, and might even be well written, but they are not put to best use. Other times, there is insufficient focus on aligning everyone's behavior across the enterprise with (civil) conduct that will support the organization's mission and goals. In yet others, leaders are not trained to prevent, detect and deal with incivility, and neither is staff. And in a disturbing proportion of cases, performance appraisals do not provide effective accountability checkpoints, nor are exit interviews designed to pick up cultural problems or specific hot spots.

Applying wrong solutions is another common problem. Well-meaning organizations employ a variety of strategies to deal with incivility, but not necessarily at the right time or in the optimal sequence. For example, frontline staff training is a great solution for building competence in civility among rank and file employees; however, if you have entrenched incivility on a particular team, bringing in a trainer for a one-time event to teach staff about civility or to go over the harassment policy is not the right solution. In this situation (as we always tell prospective clients who want to engage us for training under such circumstances), the right solution is to build the unit's leadership competence to prevent and manage incivility; building internal capacity is what is necessary. That can be done through methods such as coaching or leader-specific training. Only after that is done should staff-focused solutions such as training be considered.

In our *Canadian HR Reporter* survey on incivility,[22] we inquired about the solutions that organizations implemented to deal with incivility. Only 17 percent said that they were able to create an overall strategic organizational response. This should come as no surprise, because a strategic response requires much effort as well as buy-in from higher organizational echelons, who are often preoccupied with priorities that they perceive as more pressing. Instead, we learned from our respondents that organizations take what I would label as a path of less resistance: A whopping 69 percent reported that they "revised policies" to deal with incivility-related challenges. The problem is that policies are just the beginning of a solution: Rewriting them looks good and feels like action is happening and it also protects the organization from an accountability perspective; however, this solution rarely solves the problems on the ground.

About one-half of our respondents told us that they brought in training for management and/or frontline staff, but very few (7 percent) engaged in other initiatives such as creating team norms where employees consensually decide on principles that will guide their work together (more on team norms in chapter 12).

There is much more that an organization can do to create effective organizational processes and solutions; we will outline those in chapter 6, as part of the discussion about organizational window-fortifying strategies.

UNCIVIL ORGANIZATIONAL CULTURE

Sometimes incivility is embedded in the culture, as described earlier in the section pertaining to States of Incivility Disease. In these workplaces, incivility is expressed on a regular basis between individuals and teams, and everyone accepts that "this is how we do things here." Even new employees who enter the organization inclined to be civil get inducted into the culture and begin behaving like everyone else. Incivility is here to stay, and the multitude of costs that it exacts on the business and its people, as detailed earlier in this chapter, go unnoticed.

In such circumstances, it is practically impossible for any individual leader to create meaningful change at the team level. If you begin holding your people accountable for those seemingly insignificant rude behaviors that are accepted (or even modeled) by the manager across the hallway or by the vice president or CEO, you are bound to encounter strong resistance and your efforts will likely fail.

It is difficult to pinpoint why some organizational cultures develop in ways that result in a pervasively uncivil culture. But as you may have noticed, in certain sectors incivility tends to be more common. For example, in industries where macho or rough behavior has been the tradition and where promotion has often depended on one's ability to be crude or play the drillmaster role, incivility still abounds. Here's an example from my own journey that I always recall with great fondness:

In one of the most feisty "respectful workplace" sessions I ever delivered, I found myself in a room filled with thirty men, all dressed in orange work overalls. These men performed highly skilled and dangerous utility work outdoors. They were on the rough side, and they sure made me work hard, challenging every notion I was presenting with great fun for all, myself included.

At some point I posed the following question to the group: "Let's take a quick show of hands. What type of team would you like to be part of: Team A, where every day is like a day in the old Wild West, with people using profanities, telling racist jokes, putting others down and calling each other offensive nicknames; or would you like to work for Team B, where there's lots of fun but of the clean kind, and people are supportive and civil with each other?"

Well, about 70 percent of the men raised their hands to demonstrate a preference for Team A. I clearly had not made my case and, as a former lawyer, I should not have asked a question to which I was not certain to receive the answer I was seeking!

(Incidentally, those same men indicated that when they visited the main office, away from their male-dominated fieldwork and into the land of managers and predominantly female administrative staff, they did not use their habitual behaviors and instead engaged in impeccably respectful conduct.)

Another type of organization that is prone to develop an uncivil culture is one where there are certain groups of employees who possess a very high level of expertise, training or education on which the organization relies to fulfill its core reason for existing (think doctors in hospitals, lawyers in law firms, investment advisers in brokerage firms, physicists in nuclear plants). Sometimes in these environments, a hierarchical caste system is built right into the organization's culture. In this two-tier system, those expert employees are perceived to be of ultimate importance, and everyone else is secondary in status and voice. In some of these organizations, a gender element adds to the problem: If administrative staff consists mostly of females, and the privileged group is male-dominant, this gender imbalance exacerbates the already skewed organizational DNA. These circumstances are fertile ground for the development of a chronically uncivil culture.

We will spend some time later (in chapter 6) on the broader picture: How to create a robust, civil culture across the organization, and how to fix things when the culture falters. However, the book's focus is on what you as a leader in the trenches can do about workplace incivility—meaningful action you can take within your immediate spheres of influence, regardless of what is going on elsewhere in the organization; therefore, we will spend most of our energy together on working through a set of specific strategies and tools that will help you do exactly that, successfully.

INCIVILITY AT THE TOP

When the senior leadership is uncivil, incivility will fester throughout the organization. I could write a separate volume on the many instances where Bar-David Consulting was approached to provide consulting or training services, only to discover that some or all of the people occupying senior positions are themselves models of uncivil behavior. Indeed, in our 2011 *Canadian HR Reporter* survey,[24] we found that a majority of the comments pointed to senior managers as often being the biggest offenders. As one respondent put it, "It's hard to do anything about it when leaders don't realize that their own behavior hinders the organization."

When this is the case, incivility in the senior ranks sets the tone for what is expected and acceptable across the board. Any well-meaning manager or human resources professional who wishes to boost civility will find it to be a Sisyphean task. After all, why would anyone believe that the organization is committed to civility when a senior person is blatantly allowed to be uncivil, with no apparent ramifications?

In family-owned businesses, where the uncivil boss (or the boss's wife, husband, son or daughter) owns the business, incivility will persist for as long as this owner continues to hold the reins. When suffering individuals who work in such organizations approach me for advice on handling the situation, I tell them that they really have two viable options: let go of their upset and accept the reality, or leave the organization altogether. I wish there were better options, but I don't really see any.

Sometimes senior management is generally civil; however, there is one (or more) person on the team who is perceived to be downright abrasive. I use the term "abrasive" leader to describe a person in a leadership position whose interpersonal style causes distress to others and disrupts the work environment.[25] Abrasiveness often includes habitual uncivil practices such as belittling, dismissing, raising one's voice or using excessive sarcasm. In these cases, the incivility is tolerated because the value of this person's talents is perceived to outweigh any drawbacks related to his or her problematic interpersonal style. Therefore, those who have the power to hold this person accountable do little to change the situation. Their inaction is supported by unhelpful beliefs, such as "The abrasive style is a crucial component of the person's success" or "You can't teach an old dog new tricks; the manager simply can't change" or "Those who complain about the manager's style should acquire a thicker skin. They should stop complaining and focus on real work." Afraid of confrontation or of losing a stellar performer, senior management bury their head in the sand or have "frank discussions" that fail to set clear boundaries and consequences. None of this really works.

Working as a coach who helps organizations turn the behavior of abrasive leaders around, I can relay that these folks are capable of changing and becoming more civil. However, to get the change to happen, the organization first needs to be willing to send a very clear message to the manager: You need to change or there will be meaningful consequences.

I wish I were able to offer decisive solutions for fixing the problem of incivility in the top ranks. Unfortunately, this challenge is extremely difficult to tackle, and practically impossible if you are not in a senior position yourself (even then, it might be close to impossible for you to effect change). Often, real change happens only when a new person to take the helm as head of the organization.

However, I can promise that, starting in chapter 6, you will find an abundance of strategies that will help you navigate the waters of incivility successfully, even in these challenging circumstances. We will discuss how you can give feedback to your own uncivil boss and how to respond to incivility that is otherwise directed at you. And remember: Even when senior leadership is not modeling the desired behavior, you can still create for the team or teams that you lead a different kind of universe—one that is governed by courtesy, respect and civility.

LEADERS' OMISSIONS, MISTAKES AND OVERSIGHTS

Leaders' inability to act intelligently, decisively and effectively is a key reason incivility persists in organizations despite its numerous damaging effects. Here are the eight most common ways that leaders fall short:

1. They Engage in Uncivil Behaviors Themselves

Leaders modeling incivility is one of the biggest contributors to the creation and maintenance of workplace incivility. When the manager is uncivil, a strong message is sent: Here's how we do business around here. Furthermore, he or she has no moral authority in correcting other people's behavior. Any attempt to do so inevitably creates cynicism and resistance.

2. They Don't Trust Their Inner Canary

You've been there: you've observed an interaction between two people and your gut—your inner canary—told you that a basic line has been crossed, from decency to incivility. When leaders ignore their canary and proceed to take no action, they are enabling the problem, especially when others observe them doing nothing. Here again, a powerful message is inadvertently communicated: It's okay to be uncivil, leadership doesn't care about it one iota.

3. They Lack Diagnostic and Intervention Skills

If you've picked up this book, you may have done so because you realize that you need additional instruments in your toolbox. Indeed, managers' lack of skills to identify incivility correctly and intervene appropriately serves to keep the problem alive and well. Well-equipped leaders handle incivility early and effectively. Ill-equipped leaders become enablers.

Often, leaders like you take action but (unfortunately) it is the wrong action for the situation. For example, you may correct behavior using a very light touch, where you may have needed to take a much stronger stand to be effective, or vice versa. Or you might call a team meeting and emphasize the need for everybody to be respectful of other people's different perspectives when what you really should have done is called aside the true culprits and held them accountable for their dismissive body language. As a result, your well-intended intervention does not yield the desirable results. Stay tuned—later in the book we will explore the universe of potential strategies you can use and help to decide which ones you ought to select under different circumstances.

4. They Don't "See" It

Even though incivility takes place in his or her immediate surroundings, the manager does not register it as problematic. There are many reasons for this, such as:

- The manager doesn't physically see it because he or she is not there when it happens.
- They attribute it to personality rather than to outright rudeness.
- They personally do not take offense at the behavior in question, so they cannot see how someone else would.
- They have a personal relationship with the uncivil person and cannot see their faults.
- They have become acclimatized to the uncivil behavior because it is pervasive or built into the culture. It doesn't register in their mind as problematic because it is everywhere.

Without seeing, there is no awareness, and without awareness, a manager cannot take action.

5. They Confuse Intent with Impact

In many situations, managers don't take action because they believe that the person who initiated the incivility did not intend any harm. They avoid intervening even when there is evidence that the behavior has already had a negative impact on others. In other words, in determining whether certain behavior requires action on their part, they place more weight on the intent than on the impact factor. The result is that many incivility situations go unaddressed because the manager has determined that there was no mal-intent.

When a person behaves in an uncivil manner, it is your responsibility as a manager to deal with it, regardless of whether or not the person intended harm. This is not to say that you would disregard the issue of intent altogether. After all, there is a big difference between someone who in the course of an otherwise collegial conversation makes a joke that hits the wrong note and someone who makes it a habit to make disparaging comments in front of important stakeholders. The person's intent (to the extent that one can ever fully know another person's intent) should be factored in only when it comes to determining the course of action that you should take. Until then, what matters is only whether the behavior would be considered by the persons involved (or by any reasonable person) as uncivil. And if it is uncivil, it's important to take some kind of action, no matter what the intent was.

6. They Think It's a Diversity Issue

I often get asked, "But what about behaviors that seem like they are uncivil, but really are culturally based habits?" Underlying this question is the notion that uncivil practices that are anchored in a person's culture are legitimate, and that a manager should not tackle them, in case they step into a human rights minefield.

Actually, every single culture has teachings that follow what is known as The Golden Rule: Treat others like you wish to be treated. It existed, for instance, in ancient Babylon, China, Greece, Rome, and Persia, as well as within the teachings of Judaism, Christianity, Islam, Buddhism, Baha'i, Confucianism and Hinduism. Therefore, ascribing rudeness to cultural practices reflects flawed thinking.

Having said that, differences in communication patterns across cultures can in some cases lead to the perception of incivility—for example, when a person comes from a culture where providing very direct feedback is the norm. Applying this practice in a culture where politeness and indirectness are prime values can be perceived as overly blunt and, therefore, uncivil. In these instances, the leader should help educate the person to the local or organizational culture so that they can conduct themselves in a manner that is congruent with the organizational norms. It is legitimate to require the person to adapt their behavior to the workplace expectations related to civil conduct. Conversely, when a leader justifies uncivil behavior by attributing it to cultural diversity, he or she is condoning and perpetuating a culture of incivility.

The speaking of a foreign language on the job, especially in the presence of others who do not understand it and who might feel excluded, raises the diversity issue too. Different jurisdictions handle the language issue from different perspectives; that is, individual countries, provinces and states take different approaches, through legislation or court decisions, for example, to how language is handled in the workplace. Some have a heavy bent toward speaking only the official language of the land, while others view it as a human rights issue, maintaining that employees have an innate right to speak their mother tongue on the employer's premises.

Speaking a foreign language in the presence of those who can't understand it goes against the fundamental principle of inclusion. In fact, it triggers exclusion and alienation. Regardless of the jurisdiction or the organization's specific approach to speaking a foreign language, when a manager fails to find constructive ways to address the matter, the result is damaging on several fronts. Researcher Orly Dotan-Eliaz and her colleagues found that when they asked a group of people to perform tasks together where some reverted to another language, targets of linguistic ostracism reported more rejection and anger, less attraction toward their coworkers and even lower perceived team potency. This was true even though the people who were speaking the foreign language were otherwise socially inclusive and reverted to their language only on occasion.[26]

7. They're Afraid to Take a Stand

It takes courage to address incivility head-on, especially if it is embedded in the culture or when you need to tackle a chronic offender. Fear of taking action is rooted in many potential sources:

- General aversion to conflict
- Fear of getting into problems with the union
- Anxiety about opening a diversity-related Pandora's box
- Anxiety about not being liked
- Concern about not knowing exactly what to do
- Worry about potential boomerang effects
- Fear of ruining the relationship
- Fear of taking action that will not be supported by higher-ups

With all these potent worries looming in the background, it is no wonder that many leaders are crippled by them. It is easier to avoid and procrastinate than it is to do what needs to be done. The second part of the book is dedicated to practical tools and hands-on strategies and, as such, it will equip you with dozens of ideas to help you move beyond fear and into the land of confident action. You will discover specific phrases to use (and some to avoid), as well as when and how to use which strategies, and how to anticipate and plan for situations that may have been the cause of fear and anxiety up until now.

8. They Mishandle Complaints

All too often, managers don't take civility-related complaints seriously, or expect complainants to solve the problem on their own, even when managerial intervention is required. Other times, they take initial action in relation to the complaint, but don't follow up to ensure that change is lasting. Or they tell complainants that they should "get a thicker skin," or they might say, "I can't really do anything about that because one can't change someone's personality." The mishandling of complaints often stems from misguided underlying beliefs (which we will begin tackling in the following chapter). Other times, complaints are mishandled because the manager does not fully grasp the impact that incivility has on people and the work, or what his or her responsibilities are in this regard—all of which will also be discussed in depth in the book's second part.

MANAGEMENT-UNION ISSUES

When union and management collaborate to boost civility, a great deal can be accomplished. Unfortunately, all too often, compromised relations between management and the union (or unions) contribute to the persistence of incivility. Rather than seeing the taming of incivility as a management-union win-win, each party does its own thing. They don't work together on viable solutions that are in everyone's interest.

When the relationship between management and union is not collaborative, incivility grows like wild weeds in the cracks. Sometimes it is management that deals with union reps in ways that are uncivil, or management dismisses union concerns about abrasive conduct by leaders. Other times, individuals who hold union positions abuse their legitimate powers and treat a manager, or even a management group, in uncivil ways. I have seen situations where such individuals address management using foul or belittling language, slam doors, stomp out of meetings, publicly make sarcastic comments about a leader, uninvite managers to staff celebrations and even send threatening emails. Management is afraid to take on these uncivil individuals because of their union position, even when it is clear that the line between legitimate labor-based disagreement and outright disrespect has been crossed. Often, by the time management realizes it has to take action, the situation has become entrenched and deeply damaging to the work environment.

IMPLEMENTATION CLINIC

Leaders' Omissions, Mistakes and Oversights

The responsibility for creating a civil work environment lies in your hands as a manager. Here are some traps into which you may have inadvertently fallen:

- You didn't "see" the incivility.

- You modeled incivility.

- You didn't trust your inner canary.

- Your diagnostic or intervention skills fell short.

- You confused the person's intent with the impact it had.

- You thought it was a diversity issue instead of an incivility issue.

- You were afraid to take action.

REFLECTION
Select three of the above bulleted items that most pertain to you:

1. _____

2. _____

3. _____

Now, think of a specific circumstance that applies to each of these three items and consider the questions on the following page.

(continued)

1. How did the three items you selected impact the way that you handled the situation? (Example: "I didn't 'see' the incivility because I had known the person for many years and was used to the behavior.")

2. What were the implications of your approach or behavior—
   - For the people involved?
   - For your team?
   - For the business?
   - For you as a leader?

3. What would the problem at hand look like if it were managed better?

4. If you could have three great thinkers come to your aid in this matter, who would they be? What would they advise you to do?

5. What is one thing that needs to happen in order for you to do better next time?

6. Who would be the first to notice the change in you? What would he or she notice?

* * *

5

BLINDING BELIEFS THAT ENABLE INCIVILITY

....

UNDERLYING BELIEFS AND WORKPLACE INCIVILITY

Question:
What is the common denominator among the following?
- *Boys will be boys.*
- *Nick's rough behavior is part of his stellar sales record.*
- *What happens in Vegas stays in Vegas.*

Answer:
All three are beliefs that sanction questionable behaviors.

"Boys will be boys" is the time-honored mantra that enables schoolyard bullying. Saying that Nick's abrasiveness is crucial to his success permits the organization to turn a blind eye to the distress that the behavior causes. And the Vegas notion has protected many a wild behavior from scrutiny, and sanction.

Any group of people who work together develop a set of shared beliefs that shape how they relate to one another and how they conduct themselves in the work environment. These beliefs are sometimes shared overtly; however, they often percolate under the surface. An example of a shared belief that shapes behavior is a workgroup's belief that a good office is one that is filled with laughter and fun. Walking into this environment, any outsider would see this group engaging in laughter, fun activities and the occasional prank. If you happen to be sad or come to work in a quiet mood, you're expected to snap out of it—being in this mood violates the common understanding of how people should behave when they are part of this team.

The problem is that, in some cases, team members share beliefs that inadvertently enable and even sanction uncivil behavior, just as the "boys will be boys" assumption prevents otherwise astute adults from recognizing that little Johnny is actually a violent bully. Over the years, I have come across underlying beliefs that are the root cause of chronic damage to the work environment. In fact, much of the persistence of workplace incivility is attributable to such beliefs. These viewpoints are accepted as truth, without anyone (including the manager) ever stopping to question them or examine their negative effects more closely. When a group buys into a deep-seated belief system, its members accept conduct that they otherwise would not. It is as if everyone has blinders on, preventing them from seeing uncivil behavior for what it is.

SIX BELIEFS TO WATCH FOR

Let's examine a few commonly held beliefs that drive the behaviors of teams and/or their leaders and result in the sanctioning of uncivil conduct. As you read through them, ask yourself: To what extent do these ideas inform what you think, feel and do (or perhaps feel *unable* to do)? To what extent do people on the team hold these beliefs, and how does that shape their behavior?

We're Like a Family Here

At the heart of the we're-like-a-family-here belief lies the notion that the closeness and caring that characterize family life allow members of the workplace family to cross colleagues' personal boundaries without being hurtful or inappropriate.

Well, here's a thought: Most if not all families are flawed entities. They are not idyllic structures imbued with nothing but love and support. Some families can cause their members intense pain. And in those work environments that are fraught with incivility (or harassment, or bullying), people use the family analogy as window dressing that permits them to treat each other rudely, sarcastically or in otherwise destructive ways. The family notion stops accountability at the door.

My recommendation: In the workplace, keep the worthy parts of family—such as connection, support, informality—and decisively weed out the counterproductive parts.

From a leadership perspective, I suggest practicing extra care when you encourage your people to think of the workplace as a family. Fostering close bonds among employees is both laudable and useful. However, touting the family notion will lead you into risky terrain in a hurry. It can inadvertently erode your people's sense of safety. In response to a blog I wrote on this topic, one reader wrote, "I always felt uneasiness at hearing that 'We're like a family here' coming from management. I like to know that there are boundaries where I work and that there should be respect and a level of professionalism."

We Have the Right to Vent

You may have noticed that people hold onto their right to vent as if it were one of the Ten Commandments. They use it to justify uncensored bad-mouthing of colleagues and managers behind their unsuspecting backs. Employees and managers alike tell me that venting is a legitimate way to release steam. They say that there's a lot of stress in the workplace, and when a colleague does something frustrating or upsetting, the best way to handle it is by going to another colleague (or several, why not?) to express their authentic frustration.

Doing so has a cleansing effect that enables them to return to their work relieved and relaxed.

Here's my take on this belief: We are not machines that require the release of steam to operate properly. We are living organisms, and our actions can cause much distress to fellow living organisms. In the workplace, if a person is frustrated with a colleague, it is incumbent upon them as an adult and as a professional to handle the issue and those feelings in ways that do not involve spreading incivility and hurtful gossip. Need to vent? The place to do it is at home with your husband, dog or friend, or by tapping into professional resources, such as the employee assistance program, professional counseling or stress management programs.

I Know My Colleagues' Boundaries

Several years ago I facilitated a harassment session in an organization that qualified as a Wild West environment. Incivility was rampant, along with many as low-level harassment behaviors. One of the participants in this session, a miniature-sized, spirited female employee, referred in passing to the large-framed male sitting beside her as "fatso." When I paused to inquire about this, she explained that this colleague was her close pal and that she had obtained his permission to call him fatso five years earlier, when he first joined the team. I probed further, asking her whether calling him by that name may have perchance made him uncomfortable. She replied that she knew her friend very well and, therefore, she knew exactly which lines not to cross.

Sensing that the room was ready for further exploration, I decided to seize the moment and turn it into a meaningful learning opportunity. I turned to the man and asked him whether he was comfortable being called fatso. A long pause ensued.

Then he said, "No, I'm not comfortable at all. In fact, I don't like it one bit and never did."

People often claim that they know their colleagues' sensitivities and therefore they are able to decipher which lines not to cross. The truth is that this belief is used to allow people to say and do things that are offensive, uncivil and sometimes outright prejudiced. In short, this belief enables incivility.

And by the way, thinking that you know your colleagues' sensitivities is an illusion. In fact, I would venture to say that one knows very little about one's fellow coworkers, even those whom you've worked with for many years.

You Can't Change Someone's Personality

Monique, a bright-eyed young employee, approaches her manager to raise an issue she has with George, who works in the cubicle beside hers. A veteran employee, George is a bit rough at the edges. Monique complains about his inappropriate jokes, the sarcastic comments, the banter at others' expense. Hearing his interactions from her cubicle, she finds it hard to concentrate. She is uncomfortable dealing with the situation herself and is requesting that something be done.

The manager responds that Monique needs to understand that George intends no harm. He adds, "Unfortunately, as much as I'd like to help, you need to understand that we're talking about someone's personality here. George will be George, and we can't really change him at his age and at this stage of the game."

The belief that you cannot change someone's personality (which I refer to as "George will be George") is one of the most pervasive mental traps into which managers fall. When you hold this belief, you inevitably proceed to sanction this person's uncivil behavior, and trigger three key effects. First, George will continue to behave in this way with impunity, thereby causing damage to the work environment, as described earlier in this chapter. Second, the behavior becomes contagious and embedded in the culture as more people emulate George's incivility. Third, people view you, the manager, as an incompetent leader, which in turn tarnishes your personal brand and erodes your overall effectiveness as a people-leader.

It is true that you cannot change someone's personality. However, as a manager you have the right and responsibility to demand that during working hours everyone behave in a professional, cordial and civil manner. It is legitimate—and desirable—to require that people check the unpleasant aspects of their personality at the door when entering the workplace, and bring into the workspace only those aspects of their personality that are gracious. People with obnoxious or abrasive personalities can set them free in their private lives. In the workplace, it's about courtesy, politeness and consideration.

Not only managers hold the belief that you can't change someone's personality; employees, too, hold that notion. When a colleague displays chronically uncivil behaviors, those who are affected by it often refrain from going to management because they think that nothing can or will be done. Instead, they leave the job, or engage in retaliatory activities.

The Characteristics of the Group (or Industry) Make It Okay

"The team I manage is all females. You can imagine how much gossip and cattiness I have to deal with every day. That's what you get when you have a bunch of women working together."

I'm sure that you've heard these kinds of comments, and maybe even said them yourself. With these beliefs, prevalent uncivil behavior is overlooked because the perceived characteristics of the group, industry or workplace make it okay. In other words, uncivil behavior is explained away by characterizing it as the norm for a particular group.

Here are some common examples:

- Gen Y employees are inseparably attached to their electronic devices; you'll never get them to stop texting during meetings.
- Miners are a rogue bunch: their rough bantering is just their way of showing affection.
- In the pressure of the operating room, there's no time for niceties.
- IT people don't have people skills. Don't expect them to be friendly.
- Investment advisers have inflated egos. With that kind of money, you can't change them.
- Physicists are missing a sensitivity gene. Don't expect them to realize when they hurt someone's feelings.

Sometimes this kind of belief boils down to the notion that incivility is simply a culturally based habit. You might recall that in the previous chapter I discussed how confusion (and anxiety) related to managing a diverse workforce can lead managers to accept uncivil behavior that would not be tolerated if it weren't framed as a cultural issue. But it's not just managers whose belief system plays a role in enabling the incivility. Coworkers also often hold onto the "it's a culturally based habit" belief and, as a result, they refrain from providing the person with constructive feedback to help change their uncivil behavior.

People Need to Get Thicker Skins

Remember Monique, the bright-eyed young employee who complained to her manager about her rough-at-the-edges older colleague George? Managers who are faced with a complaint under such circumstances typically provide some variation of the following answer:

"Monique, as you know, we can't change people's personality, so the best thing to do is for you to develop a thicker skin."

(At the same time, the manager in her or his own mind might be thinking, "You've gotta be kidding me! Just grow up, suck it up and get back to work!")

The thicker-skin belief implies that it is the responsibility of the person on the receiving end to ignore, accept or even embrace colleagues' uncivil conduct. This belief renders everyone (including you, the manager) blind or indifferent to uncivil behavior.

I hear the people-need-to-get-thicker-skins notion often from folks who have been in the workforce for many years. Many of these veterans believe that the workplace is an environment where one encounters all kinds of inappropriate behaviors and, therefore, one needs to fend for oneself, which includes developing selective deafness and blindness (and of course, some savvy combat strategies to boot). Indeed, prior to the development of antiharassment legislation, females and members of minority groups survived many an insult by developing very useful thicker skins.

You can find another manifestation of the thick-skin idea in the phrase "If you can't tolerate the heat, stay out of the kitchen." I hear this most often from staff members who have been working in a given organization for many years and who—surprise!—are themselves perceived as chronically uncivil. The hot-kitchen idea is based on the notion that a workplace is a hustling and bustling place, filled with hazards and dangers, a place that requires survival skills to avoid bad burns or dangerous spillages. In this milieu, each person is free to express himself or herself in whatever way they choose. Survival in this hot kitchen requires you to adapt to its inherent risks and not be a complainer, and, if you cannot do so, then get the hell out and go work in some sanitized workplace where there's no fun and people behave like robots.

Times have changed, and nowadays employers are increasingly accountable for creating psychologically safe work environments where people can perform at their best. The pendulum is moving away from people having to fend for themselves, toward an emphasis on employers' duty to provide a healthy work environment.

DAMAGING BELIEFS that go unchecked can be found within the team's culture, within the manager's own mind, or both. These beliefs have a way of creeping up without anyone noticing. And once they do, the blindness they instill leads to uncivil and even destructive behaviors that go unchecked. Therefore, it is crucial that you leverage the human species' unique capacity to critically examine beliefs: your own and those of the people whom you are privileged to lead. Once you do so, you can work to replace these beliefs with more helpful ones.

IMPLEMENTATION CLINIC

Examining Detrimental Beliefs

Certain beliefs enable incivility. Examining the effect of such notions on people and on the business will reduce their potency and offer new paths for action.

Below you will find a sample process for facilitating a thoughtful team discussion about incivility-enabling beliefs. This example focuses on "We're like a family here." You can adapt this approach to deal with other beliefs as well, and of course you can add, change or delete questions to suit your team's needs. You can also use it with your colleagues, or just use it yourself as a reflective tool.

Sample Discussion Questions for Examining Unhelpful Beliefs

1. In what circumstances or situations do we tend to refer to our team or organizational culture as a family?

    List all the situations where this term is used, either implicitly or explicitly. (For example, do we use it to describe the support we provide to each other during difficult times? Or perhaps we use it when giving each other feedback?)

2. When we think of our culture as a family, what positive, constructive or helpful things are we able to do (individually and as a team)?

3. What positive, constructive or helpful things are we *unable* to do when we view ourselves as a family?

4. When we think of our team culture as a family, what negative, unproductive or even destructive things do we do or say (individually or as a team) that we would not otherwise be doing or saying?

5. When we think of our team as a family, what behaviors, feelings, dynamics or other factors do we ignore or disregard?

6. Which elements of the family notion do we want to foster and maintain on our team? Which do we want to leave behind?

7. What makes this issue complex (or challenging) for us?

8. How does this belief, and associated behaviors, shape others' perceptions of our team?

9. What would it take for us to change this belief?

10. What would it take for us to change the behaviors that result from the belief that we are like a family?

11. What three key actions do we need to take (individually and as a team) over the next two months to implement our answer to question number 10 above?

WHAT WORKS?

All right, we've talked quite a bit about the advantages of workplace civility and the dangers inherent in incivility. You've learned that a civil environment ensures that your people are focused and productive, and therefore are able to work toward organizational goals at full capacity. The collaborative and supportive culture associated with civility supports innovation, teamwork, engagement and talent retention—people want to stay in a workplace that makes them feel good, and to contribute their best while there.

But the risks associated with incivility and its far-reaching effects on people, organizations and the business itself loom large, as you now well know. You may have assured yourself that things will get better over time. You may have justified your lack of intervention by telling yourself that you are dealing with professional adults and that this is a workplace, not a kindergarten. You may have decided that you are not a police officer or possibly concocted other stories that support your inaction.

But incivility will not fix itself on its own. This means that it's time to talk about solutions. It is your role as a leader to prevent and deal with it. Once you move beyond your reluctance to act, you might consider it a unique privilege to ensure that people are provided with the optimal conditions for performing at their best. You'll realize that addressing incivility does not mean that you are taking on the role of a policeman, but rather it's about making sure business gets done, and in the best way possible for all involved. Addressing incivility requires a measure of courage, and when you become attuned to the responsibility and honor that rest with you, courage will find its way into your heart and actions.

Beyond the now-obvious advantages of a civil workplace, you will also find that removing incivility will be beneficial to you personally. You will spend your time on meeting your objectives rather than on dealing with complaints. You'll be able to focus on the big, important, strategic things, like building the business, rather than on fighting fires and managing HR issues that are holding the whole team and the business back. You will enjoy spending your days in a positive environment, and you will find that bringing out the best in others brings out the best in you too.

The next part of the book will introduce dozens of strategies that will help you change the field of play significantly by boosting civility, and enable you to do confidently what you need to do about incivility: prevent it, identify it and tame it.

Are you ready for the next segment of our journey together?

PART 2

STRATEGIES AND SOLUTIONS

· · · · · · · ·

IN THIS SECTION OF THE BOOK YOU WILL DISCOVER:

- Strategies for preventing, assessing and acting to tame workplace incivility

- How to change your thinking habits so that you are better prepared to deal with anything you encounter

- How to correct uncivil behavior respectfully and effectively

- How to select the right action for any circumstance

- How to deal with incivility that is directed at you

- How to make change happen after reading this book

6

MIND THE BROKEN WINDOWS
A FOUNDATIONAL PHILOSOPHY

....

In the middle of one night
Miss Clavel turned on her light
And said, "Something is not right!"
—Ludwig Bemelmans, *Madeline*

WHAT DO BROKEN WINDOWS AND INCIVILITY HAVE IN COMMON?

Jasmine has one of those thorny personalities that make people go out of their way to avoid interactions with her, on a work-related basis or otherwise. Grumpy and moody, she'll give people the silent treatment for no apparent reason. Her morning greetings are reserved for a select few, while others are noticeably excluded. On occasion, she'll announce, "Don't bug me or ask me for anything today, I'm in a crappy mood." Her eye-rolling habits are legendary. To boot, she is a malicious gossiper and rumormonger.

In another department, Ricardo has accumulated some bad habits of his own. He berates people in public for the pettiest reasons. He is notorious for curtly shooting down any idea he doesn't like, and doesn't hesitate to claim credit for other people's work. And he sees nothing wrong with barging into meetings unannounced, without the faintest apology.

Chances are that you've encountered these types of behavior in real life, and seen the price that they exact on the work environment. The fact that the Jasmines and Ricardos of our world may not necessarily be uncivil intentionally, or the fact that it is their personality that causes them to behave in these ways, does not make it less of a threat to the organizational fabric. And it certainly doesn't make it easier for those folks who have to work alongside these people day in and day out and who are at a loss as to how to handle their behavior.

Still, you may not have found the time, strength or courage to take meaningful action.

Let's leave Jasmine and Ricardo for a moment and consider this: What if vandals broke a window in one of your neighborhood buildings, and it took ages before it was fixed? (And if you're wondering what on earth this has to do with Jasmine and Ricardo, please bear with me for a moment.)

Broken Windows Theory is a criminological theory that holds that if the window of one building in any given neighborhood is broken, it needs to be fixed immediately. If not, people will assume that no one cares. Over time, crime rates in the neighborhood will rise due to a shift in people's perception of the prevailing social order. Conversely, a clean and orderly environment sends the message that the area is regularly monitored and that criminal activity will be curtailed and addressed.

Originally developed by James Wilson and George Kelling,[27] the theory was adopted by New York's mayor, Rudy Giuliani, in his quest to create better quality of life for New Yorkers, who were plagued by rampant crime in the late 1980s and early 1990s. When he was elected as mayor in 1993, Giuliani appointed William Bratton, a committed believer in Broken Windows Theory, as his police commissioner and tasked him with using the theory to guide the city's law enforcement strategy.[28] Police began enforcing the law against a range of seemingly minor infractions, all of which until that time had been considered inevitable irritants associated with life in a big city. The police began tackling subway-fare evaders, graffiti vandals and squeegee kids, public urinators and public drinkers. Over the next decade, New York experienced a sharp decline in crime rates that many have attributed to the city's new Broken Windows policing. Following Giuliani's success, Broken Windows Theory was implemented in other communities as well.[29]

Workplace incivility is akin to that famous broken window. When incivility is allowed to occur without management's intervention, it sends a loud and clear message: No one here is watching closely, no one cares enough to take action. Once the perception takes hold that windows can be broken with no ramifications, reality will unfold in one of two main paths, neither of which is good for business or for the people who work in the organization:

- **Escalation.** When the broken window of incivility is ignored, you run the risk that what began as incivility will escalate to what I described in chapter 1 as Acute Disease. Here, uncivil behaviors escalate into harassment and even bullying. Even worse, when unaddressed, incivility can easily morph into peer-based bullying: What begins as seemingly insignificant exclusion of one team member can turn into a pattern of exclusion and marginalizing that amounts to bullying and poses a risk to the affected person's dignity and health.

- **Pervasiveness.** The second path that develops when incivility is allowed to exist without anyone bothering to fix the metaphorical window is that it becomes pervasive. Your team or organization might develop a state described in chapter 1 as Chronic Infection, as demonstrated in the following story.

Several years ago, I received a call from the leader of a regional division of a cross-Canada organization, wishing to explore the possibility of us delivering incivility training for staff and leaders. During this initial consultation it became apparent that training alone would not be a viable solution and that a significantly more comprehensive solution needed to be devised. As it turned out, for years the staff in this organization had been allowed to behave in uncivil ways, with absolutely no management intervention. It began with a few individuals, and when they were able to get away with the behaviors, others began mimicking their habits. Eventually, staff began treating managers disrespectfully. When labor difficulties emerged between management and the union, the incidents of rudeness toward management escalated. They included leaving meetings with slammed doors, openly rolling eyes at managers' actions, refusing to do work ("not my job") and openly excluding certain management members from social celebrations.

In this case, had management adopted a Broken Windows approach years earlier, things would not have deteriorated to the point that they did. In fact, by the time of my initial call with the client, two managers were on stress leave due to their inability to deal with the persistent negative behaviors that were directed at them.

Mind the Windows Strategy invites you to adopt a broken-window philosophy as your overarching, core approach to dealing with workplace incivility. Adopting this philosophy means that you address workplace incivility in its minor manifestations, well before they become entrenched as acceptable behaviors that contaminate the work environment or even lead to harassment and bullying.

Let's return for a moment to Jasmine and Ricardo, whom we met earlier in this chapter. With management not intervening, they were permitted to conduct themselves however they pleased, even at the cost of disrupting the work environment. Had management in both those cases adopted the Broken Windows approach, Jasmine and Ricardo would have been called to task from the get-go and given the opportunity to bounce back to appropriate behavior or face the consequences. Furthermore, dealing with the problem quickly, as it occurred, would also have sent a clear message to others that this kind of uncivil behavior would not be tolerated, thus stopping incivility in its tracks and preventing its spread.

FIXING WINDOWS IN AUSTRALIAN ARMY STYLE

On June 12, 2013, David Morrison, chief of the Australian Army, donned his warrior armor and hunkered down to work on fixing some seriously broken windows.

When allegations surfaced that army men distributed on the Internet material that is degrading to women, Lieutenant General Morrison posted a video on YouTube, with a personal message directed at each and every army member. If you ever wanted to see a soldier fighting for what is right, this video might just about be the ultimate example. In it he says, "The actions of these members are in direct contravention to everything that the Australian Army stands for ... Those who think that it is okay to behave in ways that exploit or demean their colleagues have no place in this army ... if that does not suit you, then get out. I will be ruthless in ridding the army of people who cannot live up to its values. The standard you walk past is the standard you accept." And finally, speaking directly to the need for everyone, regardless of their organizational status, to mind the window, he asserts, "If you become aware of any individual degrading another, then show moral courage and take a stand against it."

In November of that year, the Australian Defense Force terminated the service of six of its members, ranking from sergeant to major, who were deemed to be involved in this affair, which came to be known as the "Jedi Council" scandal.

Personal Barriers to Minding the Window

If you have refrained from taking action to deal with incivility, there must have been good reasons to do so. Or at least, you persuaded yourself that the reasons were sufficiently strong to keep you from taking meaningful action; you spared yourself the effort, thought and courage that would be required. Truth is, sometimes there are indeed viable reasons to avoid action. And when your own boss is uncivil or senior management sets a bad example, or there's no David Morrison–esque commitment to minding windows at the top, the task is that much harder. But much of the time, the obstacles to minding the windows lie within your own mind and heart.

Following are some common thoughts and ideas that prevent leaders like you from seeing that the window is broken in the first place, or from recognizing that it's your job to fix it. Earlier we looked at leaders' omissions and mistakes from a broader perspective, and here I invite you to take closer look and begin considering: Which of the thoughts described below have you personally experienced? How did these thoughts affect your decisions about taking action (or not) to mind the civility windows?

- This behavior isn't really that serious.
- As long as the customer doesn't see this, no real damage is done.
- These problems are engrained in the culture—they can't be changed.
- I can't change this alone.

- Things will sort themselves out.
- It's always been like this.
- This environment is significantly more respectful than my previous workplace.
- If I begin intervening, who knows what else I will discover?
- Doing something about it will demand too much of my already overloaded time.
- The person (or persons) behaving uncivilly is (are) too powerful for me to take on.

If you are to adopt a Mind the Windows approach to incivility, exploring your own beliefs and reasons for denying that the behavior exists or that you need to deal with it is a great place to start changing yourself—and the environment upon which you have influence.

ORGANIZATIONAL WINDOW-FORTIFYING STRATEGIES

It will be significantly easier for you to mind the windows if those windows are built in a sturdy fashion in the first place. From hiring to firing (and everything in between), civility should be on the agenda. This requires your organization to put in place policies, structures and processes that will create a strong foundation that you as a leader on the ground can leverage. Key activities could include any or all of the following:

- **Define incivility.** Arrive at a definition of incivility that suits your industry and work context, and include examples of the behaviors that fall within that definition. There are advantages and disadvantages to creating a specific policy that deals with incivility. Formal policies that attempt to overprescribe specific body gestures, social inclusion and the like are bound to be ineffective, and possibly even the subject of skepticism. However, publicizing a definition and creating a shared language is an important building block to creating a strong organizational foundation.

- **Rethink your code of conduct.** A comprehensive civility strategy requires that you update your code of conduct to reflect the organization's expectations and commitment. The code will set the tone for the expected behavior. A code will not necessarily pinpoint every desirable behavior, but it will help articulate the organization's point of view, thereby enabling managers like you to coach people to become more civil, have team-based conversations or deal with problem behavior more effectively when it occurs.

- **Leverage the values.** In some organizations, the foundational values are known by all and lived daily. In other organizations, people have no clue what those formal values are. Regardless, if your organization's values include any that are relevant to encouraging civility (such as Respect or Community), figure out how to leverage these in all that you do. If your organization has not defined its core values, it is important to do so and to make the effort to engage everyone in developing awareness of the values, and in internalizing them.

- **Embed the concept of incivility into organizational processes.** References to incivility should be woven into all organizational processes. For example, embed questions and measurements pertaining to civility (or lack thereof) into hiring and onboarding practices; add the modeling of civility and maintaining a civil environment to managers' required competencies; include specific, civility-focused items in your performance appraisal process; discuss respect and civility as part of ongoing manager-staff supervisory conversations; enforce civility and consequences for incivility in the ways you structure and discuss monetary remuneration; include questions about civility in 360-degree feedback; and inquire about the state of organizational and team civility in exit interviews.

- **Get all leaders on board.** Every leader within a division, department or organization needs to be on the same page, working from a shared understanding of what incivility is, why it is important to abolish it and the strategies that will be used for doing so. Without a uniform approach, there's a real risk of isolating courageous leaders (like you!) who do take action, potentially making them the subject of resistance and cynicism.

- **Create an organization filled with models.** Leaders from the top down need to demonstrate the very behaviors that employees will be required to follow. Yes, everyone (not just you) needs to be shipshape on their hellos, be inclusive, leave their moods at the door and demonstrate respect when providing any kind of feedback.

- **Deal with abrasive leaders.** When a person with organizational authority (or any other person with perceived power, such a star salesperson) behaves habitually in uncivil ways and causes distress to the surrounding work environment, deal with this matter early and decisively. Do not succumb to organizational denial, anxiety about dealing with this person, or fear that he or she will depart and leave an irreplaceable void. Instead, offer the person support to change (specialized coaching is one great solution). But if things don't change, let the person go; the short-term costs might seem high, but the gains are immeasurable.

- **Create team norms.** Every work unit should create and commit to its own team norms (or team charter) a document that the team members themselves develop to outline agreed-upon terms of engagement.

The people in each work unit decide together how they want to treat one another, and hold each other accountable to that documented standard. It is crucial to revisit and revise these team norms on a regular basis to ensure that they are living, breathing documents. (We will discuss team norms—what they are, how to create them and how to leverage them over time—in chapter 12, as part of the discussion about Prevention and Maintenance Touchstones.)

- **Launch ongoing, public dialogue.** Make incivility a topic of conversation and debate, both formally and informally. Discuss it in team meetings. Create task forces. Have cross-departmental debates over lunch. Institute competitions and prizes for the most civil person or team. Have teams commit to working on one specific civil behavior for a week or a month, then discuss it, learn from it and decide on the behavior to practice next. Then repeat the cycle.

- **Partner with the union.** If your organization is unionized, get the union on board. It will help boost civility across the board. Working together with the union, your chances of creating lasting change are exponentially better.

- **Provide training.** Your organization should provide both leaders and employees with civility-specific training. Leaders need to understand what incivility is and how it fits within the larger business context. They need to learn how to model it themselves and how to call people on counterproductive behavior. Employees also benefit from learning how to contribute to the creation of a civil environment, where everyone is free to perform at their best.

- **Provide tools.** Disseminate tools that people can use on the job, and provide ongoing sources for tips and strategies they can use to boost civility at work. For example, Bar-David Consulting offers such civility-focused tools in the form of on-the-job learning aids for managers and staff, as well as a team-focused civility booster. Or you can use other, more generic tools offered in the marketplace that might suit your organization's needs.

- **Measure.** Use various methods to measure the levels of civility (or lack thereof). If your organization conducts engagement or other culture-based surveys at regular intervals, make sure to include questions about civility. If you work for a smaller organization that does not have the capacity to engage in costly surveys, find other ways to measure civility informally across the board, or at least in areas that seem to have challenges on this front.

WHEN THE SENIOR LEADERS ARE THE OBSTACLES TO MINDING THE WINDOWS

We've only just begun talking about strategies, and already we need to touch on one of the toughest challenges related to creating a civil work environment—and one for which the solutions I can offer to you as a manager in the trenches are, at best, limited. Sometimes managers ask me what they should do when members of the senior leadership team habitually and publicly exhibit uncivil behaviors. Those who approach me are tormented by a strong message from their inner canary that they need to take action, but they feel helpless. They know that any attempt to change things among their own staff is bound to fail because incivility is sanctioned—in fact modeled—from the top. These managers are caught between their own responsibilities as leaders and the fact that they are not high enough in the organizational hierarchy to effect meaningful change.

I dread the moments when I face this query. I dread them because when the incivility is engrained at the top, my suggestions are few, and they will not be very satisfying to the person who is sincerely seeking workable solutions. If I had a magic wand, I would wave it on behalf of the person seeking my help. But in real life, as I see it, there are three main things you can do in this situation, and none is easy.

Option 1: Be a Change Agent. Attempting to effect change in the senior leadership is a worthwhile idea and, if it works, it is by far the superior option. However, it can be risky to do so, and fears about ramifications might compromise your ability to act.

Slow down. Breathe. Welcome the challenge. With focus and some cool thinking, you'll be able to be heard and possibly even get some change going.

Here are some options to consider:

- Study the facts carefully. Usually it is no more than a handful of senior leaders (and often only one or two when you get right down to it) whose behavior is uncivil, perhaps even abusive. This means that most others are likely as upset and helpless as you are and might be willing to finally take action.

- If your organization has a code of conduct, read it carefully. Use the information as you try to change the status quo. Review the relevant respectful workplace policies too.

- Document the observed behavior and its impact in detail: what happens, when, where, with whom.

- Seek help from your human resources department or other relevant representatives.

- If you belong to a union, explore what is possible using this venue.

- Seek support from your direct manager.

- Raise your concerns with one or more persons who belong to the senior leadership team.

- If your organization has a board of directors and you are able to find a way to access the board, alerting the right people to the problem might be a viable option.

Option 2: Accept the Situation. If necessary, continue working for your employer, accept that things at the senior levels will not change (at least for now) and do your best to effect change within the areas that are within your spheres of control or influence. Beware of compromising your principles, values or soul over the long haul. Check in with yourself from time to time to ensure that you are still operating from a place of inner integrity.

Option 3: Move On. Sometimes the best solution is to leave. Take your skills, experience and integrity and go elsewhere.

And what if it is your own boss who is uncivil? We will deal with the trials and tribulations associated with this challenge later on in the book, in chapter 15, which is dedicated to incivility that is directed toward you.

Table 3: The S-O-S System

> If senior leadership's practices prevent you from living out your values, use the following process to help you decide how to proceed. I call it the S-O-S System: Stop, Observe and Shift.
>
> **Stop:** The *Stop* step requires you to heed the warning signs your inner canary is chirping about and pause. Warning signs can include a persistent feeling that something is not right, or a sense of chronic frustration and helplessness related to your inability to take meaningful action that is congruent with your values and vision. You might even be experiencing physiological stress symptoms, anxiety, withdrawal and an overall decline in performance.

(continued)

> **Observe:** At the *Observe* step, you take an honest, hard look at reality. Ask yourself tough questions, such as: What's actually happening to and around me? What specifically is troubling me? What are the chances of change happening? If I stay here, how will this affect me?
>
> **Shift:** Once you've observed and gained insights into the situation, it's time for the *Shift* step. Sometimes the shift is dramatic, requiring courage and significant risk-taking. Other times, it might consist of a relatively small change that makes a big impact on the state of things.
>
> In some situations, the shift involves internal work rather than the initiation of external changes. For example, you might discover that given all the variables, staying in your current position is a workable option and you can find ways to make it work while maintaining your integrity. This internal shift would liberate you from your current predicament and reestablish a sense of pride and fulfillment.
>
> Other times, the *Shift* step may require the courage to admit you're devoting your talent to an unworthy cause and then to follow this recognition with action. Yes, you might need to leave the job, but your integrity will accompany you to your next (and hopefully better suited) job.

Now that we've talked about adopting a foundational Mind the Windows approach to incivility, let's look at the strategy of Walk the Talk, where you will have the chance to consider and implement strategies for leading the way, and to model the behaviors you want to instill in others.

IMPLEMENTATION CLINIC

Mind the Broken Windows—
An Overarching Philosophy

According to Broken Windows Theory, when a neighborhood window is not fixed expeditiously, crime rates will rise. Similarly, when incivility is not addressed early and decisively, it will either escalate to harassment and bullying, or it will spread like a contagious disease.

As a leader, adopt a Mind the Windows approach. This lens will make it easier for you to take action—and take it early.

1. As you reflect on your organization as a whole, what broken windows currently exist that need to be fixed? Make a list.

2. What beliefs, practices and policies prevent people from taking action to fix the windows? Where do your personal beliefs and actions fit within this larger picture?

3. As you reflect on your own team, what broken windows currently exist that need to be fixed? Make a list.

4. What prevents you from taking action to fix the windows in the domains where you have the power to change things? Make a list.

5. Reflect on the items you listed in response to questions 3 and 4 above and consider: If you are to begin minding the windows more actively, what will be the first step you will need to take? The next step? The step following that step?

6. On an organizational level, what can you personally do to construct stronger windows or fix them more quickly? What challenges might you encounter once you decide to take action?

IMPLEMENTATION CLINIC

Leveraging Your Code of Conduct

In many organizations, "our values" are nothing but a collection of big words hung on a wall behind the receptionist's desk, while respect policies gather dust on HR's desk.

The effectiveness of your organization's code of conduct (if you have one) depends solely on how you use it. If you are serious about creating a civil workplace, here are some suggested ways for you to leverage the code of conduct's power on a regular basis, so that it becomes a useful and vibrant tool:

1. **Daily (or weekly) practice:** Invite team members to commit simultaneously to daily or weekly practice of one code of conduct behavior at a time. For example, if you have a daily or weekly meeting, such as a shift transfer or status update hub, take a few minutes to choose a behavior that everyone will practice diligently for a specific period of time. Make this exercise more fun and engaging by adding an element of catch-your-colleague-doing-the-behavior. Public acknowledgment or prizes are a nice additional touch.

2. **Orientation:** When new members join the team, even if only on a temporary basis, orient them in a face-to-face conversation to the code of conduct and why it is important. Answer any questions they may have. And no, having them read and sign it on a computer screen as evidence that they will follow it is not good enough.

3. **Performance appraisals:** Attach a copy of the code to the performance evaluation documents and use it as part of providing feedback on the aspects of the job that pertain to attitude or professionalism.

4. **Performance management:** In any discussion where an employee needs to be held accountable for unacceptable behavior, review the document together and discuss how the person's behavior deviates from the expected standard.

* * *

IMPLEMENTATION CLINIC

Four No-No's for Newly Appointed Leaders

If you are a freshly minted leader (or, in fact, anytime you take on responsibility for a new team), you will need to tend to broken-window matters. Use the tips below to apply the Mind the Windows approach in these circumstances.

1. Don't lose your eyesight

As a newcomer, your biggest asset is your clear eyesight and untainted inner canary. With your fresh set of eyes, you will see clearly all those workplace issues around respect, incivility and other problem dynamics that prevent the team from excelling and your stakeholders from getting the best service. Your sharp eyesight will show you where the team culture is skewed, where things are happening that should not be happening, how the work is affected by incivility and where the term "respectful workplace" is nothing but an empty phrase.

This gift of clear vision will be helpful to you, to the team and to the organization. Like Hans Christian Andersen's boy in "The Emperor's New Clothes," you will be able to question habitual perceptions of reality that are accepted as truths. And along with that you will be well positioned to suggest new (and hopefully better) ways of doing things. Some prudence, of course, might come in handy. After all, not everybody likes it when a new smart aleck appears in town, nor does everyone appreciate changes that will rattle the familiar status quo.

Your unobstructed eyesight and perceptive inner canary will lose their edge over time unless you diligently protect them from doing so. It's simply human nature for this to happen. As you get acclimatized, you will over time get inducted into the culture and lose your common sense and fresh judgment, and with it your ability to contribute a useful new perspective.

Remember that in your new role, it is your responsibility and privilege to create a civil work environment where every person can perform at his or her best, free of anything that compromises their dignity.

2. Don't succumb to New Supervisor Confusion Disease

Taking on a supervisory or managerial role requires you to make many changes and acquire numerous new skills. One shift that is not often talked about is a psychological shift: from now on, your unmitigated allegiance is to the organization. You are now operating as the organization's long arm and its representative, and it is your job to bring to life the organization's values and mission in every decision you make and any initiative you take on.

This shift in allegiance means that you might need to give up or tone down friendships that you built before you were promoted. Don't succumb to the belief that you can maintain your old friendships as if nothing has changed. If you are friends with some of your employees and visibly show it, that will inevitably create the impression of favoritism and exclusion among the others. And, as you already know from reading earlier parts of this book, when people feel excluded, their body secretes stress hormones, their concentration is compromised and the brain's pain center gets activated. None of this is good news for anyone involved (including you).

3. Forget about being popular

When you take on a leadership role, it's no longer about being liked, it's about being respected. As a leader, you will need to take actions that will decrease your popularity in the short term but over the long term will earn your staff's respect. This is especially true if you were promoted from within the team, because you will need to deal head-on with many of the problematic behaviors that you had observed while you were just one of the team. Bottom line: Being liked is a nice-to-have, but being respected is a must-have. If you want to be popular, get that need met elsewhere.

*   *   *

7

IT ALL BEGINS WITH YOU
WALK THE TALK

....

Now don't be rude
And don't be rowdy
Tell your lovin'
Partner "Howdy!"
—Dennis Lee, "Doh-Si-Doh," *The Ice Cream Store*

A manager was referred to me for coaching after an internal workplace investigation labeled him as abrasive. As it turned out, this manager was extremely uncomfortable with people, private and anxious. He had learned over time to adopt some social mannerisms that helped him overcome some of these traits, but as a result of his natural tendencies, he often did not greet people with hello, and in his interactions he came across as cold and distant. During times of excessive stress at work, he would become even less social and skip the small, learned niceties that he had adopted. In these circumstances, he would use short sentences, expressed in a very tense tone. He found comfort in maintaining a close relationship with one of the employees who reported to him, whom he had trusted from the days before he was promoted to manager of the unit.

Over time, the team grew to think of this manager as harsh and uncivil. In typical spiral effect fashion, they would spend significant work time *talking about him behind his back. Several people engaged in small, carefully crafted retaliatory actions toward him, and the colleague with whom he was close began being excluded from social activities and occasionally even work-related issues. All this time, the manager was very pleased with his own performance, while telling himself that people understood and accepted his introverted nature.*

The manager was, therefore, understandably shocked and devastated when the internal complaint was launched, alleging preferential treatment of his friend and ally, and revealing the other allegations of repeated incivility. It took thorough examination of the situation, including intensive coaching and implementation of real changes, to alter the course of this leader and his team.

A civil workplace environment begins with you, the leader. It's not enough to talk the talk, you actually have to *walk* the talk, day in and day out. You are the model and the standard that people should be able to look up to. If your own behavior is uncivil, you will lack the moral authority to require others to behave in a civil fashion. In fact, if people perceive you to be uncivil, any changes that you attempt to make to the environment will be perceived as hypocritical and will lead nowhere in a hurry.

Just like any corporation, you too have a personal brand, and your personal brand should spell "civility." So the first step in boosting civility in your work environment begins with examining your own behavior and making necessary changes to ensure that your personal brand is squeaky-clean.

INCIVILITY AND POWER

When people in power are uncivil, things take on a whole different flavor than when incivility is performed by colleagues. First, as in any other power structure, those who are lower on the totem pole observe those above them much more closely than they observe people at the same level. As such, a person is much more likely to notice when a manager plays favorites or makes a critical comment than one would if it were a colleague doing so. Uncivil behavior from a manager affects us deeply, as we find ourselves worrying and obsessing about an incident much more than if this behavior had been displayed by any old colleague.

Pearson and Porath conducted in-depth interviews across sectors in the United States and Canada and, not surprisingly, found that people in power have more opportunities to be uncivil (think public criticism or barging into meetings) and that they can get away with behaviors that others with less institutional power would not be able to.[29] The position of power and the lack of repercussions lead some managers to develop chronic uncivil habits without being challenged or held to account.

Staff who report to a habitually uncivil manager find it near impossible to let the person know how troubling the behavior is. The huge risks to doing so lead to a sense of paralysis, resulting in the employee taking no overt action. (Later on in the book I will offer you strategies for handling situations where your own manager is uncivil toward you.)

A leader who is chronically uncivil creates deep distress in the environment, triggering fear, sick leaves and departure of good people. Abrasive managers are often referred to as bullies or abusers who act with intent. But my experience working with abrasive leaders in a coaching capacity has taught me that oftentimes they are utterly unaware of their uncivil behaviors or the ways in which they use language, both verbal and nonverbal. Even if they are aware of the specific behaviors they perform, they truly cannot see how their behavior can be perceived as threatening or debilitating. In short, they suffer from significant blind spots.

The only reason that any manager is free to behave in an abrasive fashion is because he or she is allowed, enabled and possibly even incentivized to do so. When someone in the organization sets clear boundaries and holds this person accountable, things never reach this point. The problem is that the perception that someone has power prevents others in the organization (and even those who are more senior than the person in question) from taking them on. As a result, the behavior continues until it creates measurable damage, without the person having a chance to correct their behavior.

THE SELF-EXAMINATION IMPERATIVE

Anyone can behave in an uncivil manner from time to time, including you. The good news is that you can minimize your own incivility. And the even better news is that the more self-aware you are, the easier it is to identify situations where you may have been uncivil, to own your mistakes, apologize or otherwise fix them.

Begin by examining yourself with brutal honesty. Being your own worst critic will enable you to make necessary changes in yourself, and fortify your subsequent ability to effect change in others. The key areas you'll need to cover are:

1. Your beliefs, intentions and blind spots
2. Behaviors to avoid
3. Behaviors you should demonstrate

Your Beliefs, Intentions and Blind Spots

Explore your own beliefs to identify any that might inadvertently lead you to behave in ways that others will perceive as uncivil. Perform an honest scan to examine whether you hold any of the beliefs I described in chapter 5 (such as "We're like a family here," or "With all the life-and-death pressures in our environment, there's no time for niceties") or any other beliefs that may not have been mentioned but that might be causing you to behave in uncivil ways.

Then, scan your intentions: While you might have the best intentions, others might have a very different perspective on the behaviors that are associated with your good intentions. Sometimes you may not even have a specific intention when you engage in a given behavior and, therefore, you are unaware of its negative impact on others and on the way they view you. Below is a sampling of comments I hear repeatedly from well-meaning managers who are blind to the damage that they are doing to others, and bringing upon themselves:

- I'm not a morning person.
- I can't talk to anyone before I have my first coffee.
- I am shy.
- I am sarcastic by nature; it's just part of who I am.
- When there are serious deadlines, I don't have time or patience for making small talk.
- I have a natural affinity with some people on my staff, so I naturally spend more time with them.
- I've been friends with this person from the beginning, and I can't just drop that friendship now that I am in management.
- I've known these folks for so long, I can let loose and be my natural self.
- My role is very important, so I have to be connected electronically at all times, even at meetings or in conversation.

So let's take a closer look and see how others might perceive some of your intentions and actions.

Table 4: Intentions-Perceptions Traps

	Your Intention	Their Perception
1	You believe that the fastest route to self-improvement is by learning from one's mistakes. You therefore provide immediate and frequent feedback on any mistakes made by your staff.	You are overly critical and lack empathy. You dismiss everyone's efforts.
2	You are a spontaneous person and sometimes you share your thoughts in a somewhat unfiltered fashion.	You are reckless. You think that apologizing for critical and dismissive comments erases or justifies the pain that you have inflicted.
3	You are running a meeting where important decisions need to be made. There's no time to waste, so when people repeat their point after they've already said it once, you act responsibly by saying, "Okay, we've got your key points. Let's move on now."	You are an autocrat who pretends to be inclusive while really thinking that everyone else is dumb.
4	You have a lot of responsibility and therefore need to be constantly monitoring and responding to messages on your mobile device. You trust that everyone knows that you are great at multitasking, someone who can listen and text at the same time.	You are rude and self-aggrandizing.

	Your Intention	Their Perception
5	You deal with issues using wit and sarcasm. You believe these traits contribute to a lighthearted and fun work environment.	Your sarcasm is mean and hurtful. You are clueless in reading people's reactions.
6	When a client complaint comes in regarding the performance of one of your staff, you deal with it immediately. A straight shooter and problem solver, you send the staff person a short email saying, "Come see me."	You are a manager who leaps to judgment and blame. You lack basic manners and are insensitive to people's experiences and feelings.
7	You were promoted from within the team. You maintain close relationships with the two people with whom you were really close before your promotion.	You spy on team members and play favorites.
8	With so much work pressure and frustrations with people in other departments, sometimes you vent about those other people to your staff.	You are unable to regulate your emotions. You cannot be trusted.
9	You work in a high-pressure environment. When stressed, you sometimes are preoccupied and miss observing the basic niceties.	All you care about is getting the job done. You couldn't care less about your people.
10	Some people are chronically unmotivated. There are times where you really needs to get their attention, so you raise your voice slightly or speak in a strict tone to send the message that the matter at hand is important.	You are a bully who yells and shouts to get your way.

(continued)

	Your Intention	Their Perception
11	When pressure is high, you release steam by using the occasional swearword. You make sure to do it only in the presence of staff who you trust will not be offended.	You lack basic decorum. You don't know the difference between a bar and a workplace.
12	You have an important job and are often called upon to tend to things on short notice. Sometimes this leads to you being late to meetings with your staff or not showing up at all.	You think that what your staff does is unimportant. You think that you are better than everyone else. Moreover, you lack basic manners.
13	You wish that patience was one of your virtues, but the truth is that it's not. Sometimes your impatience shows through your physical reactions, but everyone knows that for the truly important things you always have limitless patience and time.	Your eye-rolling, deep sighs and impatient hand gestures are rude, discourteous and dismissive.

As table 4 demonstrates, there is no shortage of blind spots. Having blind spots is human; we all practice counterproductive behaviors that are outside our awareness. But if you want to Walk the Talk, you'll need to clean up some of the mess you might be creating. Seeking feedback from others is one of the best methods for obtaining quality data that will help you change.

Use these tips to help you collect quality feedback:

Selecting the right people

1. Choose a cross-sectional representation of people to provide the feedback: people who report to you, peers and superiors.

2. Select people who are good observers of behavior; they will give you detailed data.

3. Don't go only to those who like and appreciate you. Those who are not necessarily your fans might be great sources of information.

Setting the stage

1. Decide whether to let people know in advance that you will be seeking feedback on your incivility habits or whether it is better to do it on a spontaneous basis.

2. Let them know why you are asking for the feedback—the larger context as well as your personal journey.

3. Clarify that you are open to hearing anything they have to say, with an open mind and without becoming defensive.

4. Ask for the feedback to be as specific as possible.

5. Request their observations on your behavior as well as on the impact it has (or might have) on others.

When receiving the feedback

1. Maintain a relaxed body posture.

2. Monitor your reactions—do not get defensive.

3. Encourage additional feedback by using phrases such as "What else have you seen?" or "What do you think others might be seeing that I do not see?"

4. Ask clarifying questions to receive specific data (for example, "What specifically do you see or hear that leads you to say that I sometimes come across as impatient?").

5. Thank them for their input and candor, and invite them to let you know of anything else they may think of after the conversation.

After the fact

1. Thank people again in person, or via email, phone or a written note, letting them know what specifically you found helpful and what action you plan to take based on their feedback.

2. Proceed to make the necessary changes!

If, as a result of your self-examination, you decide to make significant and noticeable changes to your behavior, it might be prudent to let your team members know that you are embarking on a self-improvement path. Doing so will—

- Demonstrate your ability to grow and learn as a leader.
- Encourage people to take note of the process and support you on your journey.
- Provide you with the moral foundation to later ask others to change as well.
- Help you keep to your new habits because you committed publicly to changing.

Behaviors to Avoid

As you begin to examine your behavior with unrelenting honesty, you will inadvertently discover behaviors that you will need to discard. By now, you are already quite familiar with the types of behaviors that people perceive as uncivil, but just to be on the safe side, let's review the behaviors that should be top of mind to avoid at all costs.

Table 5: Behaviors to Avoid

- Eye-rolling
- Sarcasm
- A harsh tone or raised voice
- Skipping greetings
- Jokes or comments that could be perceived as offensive
- Gossip or speaking in a disapproving way of someone in his or her absence
- Profanities, swearing or otherwise offensive language
- Dismissive facial expressions and physical reactions
- Playing favorites—maintaining closer relationships with some staff but not others
- Rude use of technology of any kind
- Excessively to-the-point or critical emails
- Speaking in a foreign language in the presence of people who do not speak that language

Behaviors You Should Demonstrate

Model civility and respect through fair treatment, respectful communication, cordial behavior and considerate use of electronic devices. Following the list below will go a long way.

- When allocating undesirable tasks, make sure to maintain a sincerely caring tone.
- Avoid blaming, and own your own part in any problem that may arise.

- Greet everyone, especially your staff, with a hello or an acknowledging friendly nod, as appropriate. Remember that even the remote sense of being excluded and ostracized triggers a negative fight-or-flight reaction in the brain's anterior cingulate cortex.

- Make sure to use "thank you" and "please." The absence of these simple words, in conjunction with your institutional power, creates an impression of incivility.

- Before sending emails that are very short or that deal with potentially sensitive matters, read them as if you were the person receiving them. Add, remove or change anything that could be upsetting or misinterpreted.

- Always use a civil tone. Smiling slightly as you speak will change the way the words sound. This is especially useful on the phone. This may sound basic, but it is crucial.

- Always credit ideas to those who contributed to their creation.

- Get to know your biases—and never act on them. Having biases is part of being human, but acting on them ranges from incivility right up to illegal discrimination.

- Ask people specifically how they would like to be treated and then attempt to do so.

MANAGE YOUR STRESS LEVELS

To be a model of civility, you will need to monitor your personal stress levels. When you're stressed, you are more likely to act in uncivil ways, or to be short, discourteous or dismissive. All these will have a negative effect on your team members and on their perception of you as a leader, not to mention on their productivity and motivation.

To monitor your stress levels and prevent them from hijacking the agenda, you can adopt the S-O-S System outlined earlier, in table 3. You will need to Stop when you observe yourself manifesting stress-induced behaviors, Observe by taking a long, hard look at what's causing your stress and how you are showing it, and Shift to make the necessary small or large changes that will help you reclaim your equilibrium.

Reducing your stress will require you to apply strategies that will work for you, given who you are and the circumstances of your life. In my earlier days as a trainer and consultant, before I entered the world of workplace incivility, I delivered hundreds of lunch 'n' learn sessions focused on stress resilience and work-life balance. Through my observations, I've come to classify people's responses to stress as falling within one of the following categories:

- **Proactive Strategies.** These comprise the preventive behaviors and mental practices that fortify a person's resiliency baseline. Practicing these creates an invisible immunization of sorts, one that decreases the chance of experiencing events as stressful to begin with. Typical examples are: sleeping at least eight hours a night, viewing events with a cup-half-full approach, practicing yoga and meditation regularly, exercising and having a strong social network.

- **Responsive Strategies.** These are the strategies that people use when responding to a specific stressor (or multiple ones). For example, counting to ten before speaking is a classic responsive strategy. Other examples of healthy responsive strategies include challenging our negative thinking habits about the stressor, taking deep diaphragmatic breaths when we feel overwhelmed by an event (or by our thoughts about it), seeking support from friends or from professionals and removing the stressor by saying no.

- **Reactive Strategies.** These are the unhealthy behaviors that we engage in as a means of dealing with stress. Unfortunately, these strategies have a habit of backfiring on us. Classic examples include excessive drinking, gambling, self-medicating and overeating. As you can imagine, I do not recommend these, and certainly not for you as a manager.

The more you can do to employ proactive and responsive strategies, rather than reactive strategies, to deal with your stress, the better. Whatever it takes, do what you need to do to keep your stress levels in check. You owe it to yourself as well as to the people whom you lead.

DEFENSIVE MANAGEMENT IN A WORLD SATURATED WITH HARASSMENT AND BULLYING

You may have already noticed that over the past years there has been a spike across industries in employee complaints and legal actions related to harassment and bullying.

Four key trends directly contribute to this shift: First, increasingly visible workplace harassment and bullying legislation initiatives in various jurisdictions have put the topic on the public and corporate agenda.

Second, an increasing number of unions are including bullying-related clauses in their collective agreements, thereby raising members' awareness and requiring greater organizational accountability.

Third, awareness about teen and schoolyard bullying has reached record highs, partly due to tragic cases that have led to victims' suicide. This focus on bullying in young people's lives has had a ripple effect into the workplace.

Fourth, the terms "bullying" and "harassment" have become household terms. Bullying bosses in particular have become a hot media topic (see table 6).

Table 6: Bully Bosses in the Media

Below is a random list of article titles appearing in both hard-copy and online magazines such as *Forbes, Psychology Today,* the *New York Times,* the *Globe and Mail,* and even *Parenting*:

- Bully Bosses: Cruel Managers Make Workers Feel Powerless
- How to Deal with a Bullying Boss
- Is Your Boss Just Tough, or a Bully?
- 8 Telltale Signs of a Bully Boss
- Your Bullying Boss May Be Slowly Killing You
- Fear in the Workplace: The Bullying Boss
- How to Handle a Bullying Boss: 7 Steps (with Pictures)
- The Cost of Keeping a Bully Boss
- When the Boss Is a Bully
- How to Deal with a Difficult or Bullying Boss
- How to Deal with a Toxic Boss or Co-Worker
- The CEO Refresher: When the Boss Is a Bully
- Working for a Boss Who Bullies
- 7 Ways to Protect Yourself If Your Boss Is a Bully
- How to Cope with Bullying in the Workplace
- Smart Ways to Deal When Your Boss Is a Bully
- How to Fight Back—and Win—Against a Bully Boss Who Wants to Hurt You
- Bullying Bosses Take Toll on Employees

Even though bullying often happens between peers or, in fact, toward a manager by someone who reports to him or her, the image of the archetypical bully boss is lodged into many people's psyche. The presence of the four trends mentioned above means that there is a greater likelihood that managers will be accused of bullying, whether they deserve it or not. People like you are now faced with a new kind of risk: Hard-working, decent managers find themselves unfairly accused of bullying, thereby triggering a set of negative repercussions for themselves and for the organization.

Certain situations, by their very nature, are prone to trigger harassment or bullying allegations against you. For example, when you have to engage in performance management where you must closely scrutinize an employee's poor performance, the perception of unfair or harsh treatment may readily emerge. Or in situations requiring exercise of authority and power, even simple decisions regarding vacation or allotment of professional development days can be highly sensitive and open to misinterpretation. Or during periods of time crunches and tight deadlines, when many managers resort to authoritarian or micro-management practices, their stressed-out employees are bound to experience the demands as abusive.

In these high-risk situations, as well as at all other times, it is imperative that you maintain the highest standard of personal civility. If your style is always respectful, cordial, fair and inclusive, the likelihood of you being inadvertently slapped with a harassment or bullying complaint is significantly diminished. If you maintain an even-keeled temperament on a regular basis, then even when you have to manage someone's performance, your solid civil record will mitigate the chances of a complaint being launched against you.

My work in coaching managers who have been deemed to have an abrasive management style has taught me important lessons about the dangers of failing to understand the risks you face when you don't manage yourself well. I see (or consult about) leaders who are referred to me following a harassment or human rights complaint that raises concerns about their conduct, sometimes to the point of placing them under the threat of termination. As we launch the coaching, I set out to interview those who report to them, as well as their peers and colleagues. Here, I often learn that my clients' problems stem from behaviors that by and large consist of incivility as we have been discussing here in *Trust Your Canary*. I hear about my clients' habits of skipping some of the basics, such as saying hello to everyone equally, or using emails in a way that is perceived as curt and demanding, or treating people in dismissive ways. Even though these are low-intensity behaviors, the fact that the instigator is a person in power, coupled with the repetition of these behaviors over time, leads to allegations that could have been prevented if the manager were more aware of their own level of civility in the first place.

LEAD WITH A FOCUS ON PERCEIVED JUSTICE

In 1987, Jerald Greenberg first introduced the concept of organizational justice, and you may want to keep this theory in mind as you go about implementing the Walk the Talk strategy.

Rooted in Equity Theory, organizational justice highlights the fact that employees' perceptions of the fairness with which the organization and its decision makers treat them will shape their behavior. It's all about perceptions: Regardless of whether or not you as a leader think that you are acting fairly, if people perceive that they are treated unfairly, their attitudes and behaviors will reflect that perception.

In plain words, you need to demonstrate that you deal with people fairly, equitably and with sensitivity to the impact that your decisions and actions will have on them. If you don't, trouble looms.

Specifically, you may want to watch the ways in which you behave along the following three axes that the theory identifies as crucial:

- **Distributive justice.** This type of justice refers to the perceived fairness of distributions or allocations of rewards. In other words, the degrees to which people perceive that you are distributing "carrots and sticks" fairly. Here you find things such as promotion-related decisions, remuneration, training and development opportunities, as well as decisions about who works which shift, holiday coverage, and overtime duties.

- **Procedural justice.** This type of justice refers to the perceived fairness of the procedures used to make decisions, the voice that people have in participating in decisions that concern them. For example, was their perspective considered (even indirectly) before the decision was made? Did they have a chance to question, change or appeal a decision after it was made? Was the process that was used to arrive at the decision fair?

- **Interactional justice.** Here we look at the treatment that individuals receive as decisions are made. Are they treated with dignity, respect and sensitivity when decisions are relayed or executed? Are they given sufficient information? Does management provide adequate explanations? Is management transparent? Is information provided in a timely fashion?

When people perceive a lack of fairness on any of the above metrics, a number of consequences will occur: First, trust is eroded as people conclude that management does not live up to basic fairness principles. Second, people will take action to restore justice, by lowering their work effort (as we have seen earlier in the book) or via other counterproductive behavior, including sabotage and theft. Job satisfaction and commitment to the organization will also be affected when people perceive themselves as being treated unjustly. And you can also count on absenteeism and withdrawal to increase when people feel discouraged and distrustful.

You may have already realized when reading the above that when you, the leader, engage in seemingly insignificant unjust, rude or insensitive behavior, people will perceive you as acting in an unfair manner and they will react in counterproductive and even destructive ways. In one of the cases where I helped to rehabilitate the behavior of an abrasive leader, there were exceptionally high turnover and absenteeism levels on this leader's unit. When I interviewed people who reported to this manager, some told me point blank that when their manager makes judgments about their mistakes without ever hearing their point of view, or comes to conclusions without allowing them to explain what happened, they simply call in sick the next day. In this case, the manager's shortcomings in the procedural justice arena led to people taking action to restore their inner sense of equity and fairness in the only way they were legitimately able to do so: simply not show up.

WE'VE SEEN throughout this chapter that to Walk the Talk involves much more than first meets the eye. It encompasses modeling the desired behaviors, managing your stress levels, considering how others might misinterpret your intentions and exploring your beliefs and blind spots. It also requires you to understand the dynamics of power and how easily your actions can be perceived as bullying and why it is important to adopt fair and just management practices. But most of all, walking the talk means stepping up to the plate and being (consistently) thoughtful and kind.

IMPLEMENTATION CLINIC

Walk the Talk: It All Begins with You

Boosting civility in the work environment begins with you, the leader. Examine your conduct and change yourself before demanding change in others. To facilitate the process, reflect on the following:

1. What counterproductive behaviors do you currently practice? Review the list below and place the items in an order that reflects the frequency or severity with which you engage in these behaviors:

   - Eye-rolling
   - Sarcasm
   - A harsh tone or raised voice
   - Skipping greetings
   - Jokes or comments that could be perceived as insensitive
   - Gossip or speaking in a disapproving way of someone
   - Profanities, swearing or otherwise offensive language
   - Dismissive facial expressions and physical reactions
   - Closer relationships with some staff and not others—"playing favorites"
   - Rude use of technology of any kind
   - Excessively to-the-point or critical emails
   - Other: _____

2. What beliefs do you hold that support you engaging in your top three behaviors above?

   (Examples: that's my personality, time is precious, I have the kind of face that shows how I feel.)

   Belief no. 1: _____

   Belief no. 2: _____

   Belief no. 3: _____

3. What three steps will you take to Walk the Talk and boost your civility—over the next two weeks? Two months?

4. Will you need to communicate to others that you plan to consciously change your behavior? If so, to whom? How will you do that? What will your message be?

5. Once you begin changing your habits, what impact do you anticipate this will have on other people? On the work environment?

8

KNOW WHEN THE LINE IS CROSSED
TRUST YOUR CANARY, AND A CIVILITY LITMUS TEST

....

Mary had a pretty bird,
With feathers bright and yellow,
Slender legs—upon my word,
He was a pretty fellow.
The sweetest notes he always sang,
Which much delighted Mary;
And near the cage she'd ever sit,
To hear her own canary.
—Mother Goose, "Mary's Canary"

Adopting a broken-window philosophy—putting in place preventive measures and then dealing with uncivil behavior right away, as it happens, to prevent its spread—is the first step in taming incivility in the workplace. But how do you go about ascertaining when a window has been broken, when that line between civility and incivility has been crossed? After all, things can be so confusing, ambiguous and multilayered. Let's examine two strategies that might help: Trusting Your Inner Canary and Raising the Banner.

CANARIES IN OUR MIDST

"At their height, there were at least 3,000 of them employed in coal mines across the UK, and despite weighing just 15 to 20g, worldwide it is believed that they could have saved the lives of more than a million men."
—Neil Prior, "How 1896 Tylorstown Pit Disaster Prompted Safety Change," Wales BBC News, January 28, 2012

Earlier on, in chapter 1, we talked about how somewhere inside you resides your very own, built-in, personal canary, similar to the ones that coal miners would take into the shaft with them as a means of detecting poisonous gases.

Your canary's job is to alert you when the invisible line that separates civility and incivility has been crossed. For example, you might be taking part in a work-related conversation, when suddenly someone makes a nasty comment about a colleague who is not present. Immediately you are flooded by overwhelming discomfort, accompanied by an inability to respond in the moment. Your canary has just alerted you that there are dangerous substances in the air.

This inner compass is so crucial to the abolishment of workplace incivility that I decided to name the book *Trust Your Canary* to highlight the need for you to trust the innate reaction that leads you instinctively in the direction of doing what is right.

Your canary has had hundreds, even thousands, of years to develop its acute sensitivity. That gut feeling is the result of generation upon generation of your culture and family telling their young how to distinguish right from wrong and proper from improper. From the beginning of time, your ancestors have been telling their children, "In our family, we don't behave that way" or "Good people don't do those kinds of things" or "Go apologize to your sister right now for hurting her feelings." Through this kind of multigenerational guidance, your inner system has become extremely astute at assessing the environment and your own place within it, in ways that support harmonious living alongside other people.

Not all personal canaries are born equal, however, and their level of sensitivity varies. Some people have acutely sensitive ones, while other canaries awaken less frequently. Oftentimes, though not always, your canary's sensitivity will be shaped by your background and by your position in the societal power structures. In other words, the degree of societal privilege you enjoy might make you less or more prone to have an acutely reactive inner canary. For example, if you were raised in a privileged segment of society, your canary might be less sensitive than that of someone who was raised in more marginal parts of the culture. In Western society, if you are a white, middle-aged, middle-class, professional male, you may not be intrinsically as attuned to ostracism, injustice or power imbalances as might be, say, a young female refugee immigrant. These, of course, are sweeping generalizations; however, it is important to realize that a person might be inclined to be underreactive or overreactive to situations and that this tendency might be informed by his or her background and privilege.

As a leader, you need to be cognizant of your canary's sensitivity level as compared with that of others. If yours is not highly responsive, you may not pick up instances that other people might be reacting to, especially those who rely on you to take a leading role in maintaining civility in the work environment. This means that you might be present when problem behavior happens but you might not register the situation as problematic. Because your canary is less reactive by nature, it is unable to pick up on the cues at hand and, as a result, you might be perceived as endorsing the behavior. (For example, you might laugh at something that others find offensive.)

If, on the other hand, your canary happens to be one that makes loud alert sounds at even the smallest issue, you can find yourself overreacting to situations that, in the grand scheme of things, are best left alone. If your canary reacted, there probably was something in that incident that indeed was not quite right; however, if you respond to every situation, you might end up creating the perception of relentless policing, or simply have people tune out to your interventions. The best path is to pick your battles, and to top that up with learning to express your valid concerns in ways that people can truly hear.

Knowing how sensitive your personal canary is compared with others' canaries enables you to examine your reactions with a measure of objectivity. If you know you have a highly sensitive inner canary, you might do well to ask yourself whether the situation really warrants action on your part. If yours is a slower-to-react one, it might be prudent to consult someone who has a different perspective and get that person's take on situations when you are not sure whether or not someone else's canary would have snapped into action.

Your canary might be exceptional at picking up particular types of line-crossing behaviors but quite sluggish to pick up other types of improprieties. For example, some leaders are highly attuned to any signs of exclusion or marginalization on the teams they lead (or, for that matter, on the teams where they are members.) The minute a person is excluded by others, even in small ways, this leader's canary gets activated in a significant way and he or she knows they need to act or else they will not be at peace. On the other hand, the very same leader might be completely oblivious to the use of foul language or a raised voice.

The basic guideline I recommend that you follow is: Know thy canary. The more intimately familiar you are with it, the more skilled you will be at trusting and using it.

AN ACTIVATED CANARY MEANS ACTION

When your inner canary gets triggered in response to specific circumstances, it means that you as a leader need to take some form of action

Know When the Line Is Crossed | 147

to remedy the civility problems at hand. What you choose to do will depend on the severity of the behavior, the players, the dynamics of the situation and the overall context. The strategies that follow throughout the rest of the book will help you navigate through your many options. For now, let's review just a few key points.

Sometimes you do not observe the situation yourself but, rather, someone steps forth to complain to you about another person's behavior. In many situations you will immediately get the sense that the lines between respect and disrespect have been crossed and thus get mobilized. Other times you might think, "Hmm, that wouldn't really bother me, so it shouldn't bother that person either," and refrain from taking action. What you are essentially saying is that your own canary is not sensitive to this type of behavior and, therefore, other people should not be reacting so strongly either.

Well, frankly, that response is not good enough. Some people's threshold is not quite as high as yours; they get upset and worried and unable to work to their full potential when exposed to behaviors that may not bother you but certainly do affect them. They expect you to take some form of action, and they might have a good case. Remember that it is your responsibility to provide an environment where people can perform at their best, and if you are not sure whether the person is overly sensitive, ask a trusted colleague whether his or her canary would get activated under the set of circumstances at hand.

Relying on your inner canary becomes trickier when the situation is protracted or even chronic, as manifested in the example below.

A newly appointed, relatively inexperienced supervisor sought our services to deal with the following challenge: two women on her team had been locked in a conflict for several years. It started years earlier with minor work-related resentments, and every year a couple of new small issues were added into the pot, all of which resulted in the women not talking to each other, even though they needed to in order to do their work. They would communicate using sticky notes, which they attached to the paperwork that needed to flow between them in the course of the day. These sticky notes became problematic in and of themselves, with each woman taking offense to the way in which the other had worded her notes.

From the moment she was appointed to lead the team, the supervisor noted that her canary was sending alert signals. The previous supervisor had framed the issue as a matter of interpersonal conflict and gave up on trying to resolve it after making a couple of failed attempts at mediating between the two women. However, the new supervisor instantly felt that this was a matter of lack of professionalism that should not be tolerated in the workplace. She also immediately concluded that these behaviors were impacting productivity and work effectiveness.

Initially, the new supervisor trusted her gut completely and planned to take action accordingly. However, new to her role, she had a number of pressing priorities and left this matter on the back burner for the first while, intending to get to it once she had dealt with the other priorities.

After a while, she lost that sense of certainty. She bought into the notion that this was a legitimate conflict between two people, and let that supersede her own sense that this was not legitimate behavior in the workplace. As a result, she took no action and the problem continued to fester.

As happened to this supervisor, extended exposure to uncivil behavior, even if it initially sets your canary to tweeting an alert, eventually leads to a muffling of its sounds. What might start with a loud and persistent inner cry turns over time into a soft murmur. You become desensitized to the situation, maybe even accept it. You become partially blind (or deaf, in this case) to the problem and lose your impetus to take action.

Here's the bottom line: Trust your canary. It's one of the most critical and reliable tools that you will ever possess. It helps you identify when you must take action to restore respect and civility. As a leader in your organization, it is incumbent upon you to step up and do what's right, just as all those generations in your family and culture would expect you to do.

ONCE YOUR INNER CANARY has alerted you to the presence of a problem, you may want to use logical criteria to assess and analyze the situation, its severity and the level of response you will need to take. This is where you can apply a quick mental litmus test, in the form of the next strategy, Raise the Banner.

A WORLD OF EVER-SHIFTING LINES AND BANNERS

When I was a Grade 11 student, my classmates and I would stand around the chemistry lab table, which was overflowing with test tubes and mysterious-looking contraptions, watching our teacher generate various forms of chemical magic in front of our wide-open eyes. When he was done, and while we were all still leaning forward with our elbows on the table and our behinds sticking out, he'd deal the female student standing closest to him a little friendly slap on the buttocks and announce to no one in particular, "Okay, we're done for today, now go write up your lab reports!"

It never occurred to any of us females, or to our male counterparts, that we had a right to protest or complain to anyone about our teacher's fanny-tapping habit. If you wanted to avoid being touched, you had to devise your own self-defense strategy. And, as I quickly discovered, the best strategy was to stand at the far end of the table, well away from the teacher. That seemed to work extremely well.

Well, the times sure have changed. Nowadays, if he weren't smart enough to avoid that behavior in the first place, my dear teacher would be slapped with a sexual-harassment (or, in some jurisdictions, a physical-violence) complaint. The matter would be taken seriously and the consequences could be dire.

You already know that the line between what is acceptable and what isn't is constantly changing. The workplace is increasingly considered to be a place where people should be protected from any form of behavior that compromises their dignity. This evolution is informed by legislative changes, court and arbitration decisions, occupational health and safety policies, collective agreements and academic research findings.

The workplace pendulum is moving in one direction, and its movement is becoming increasingly rapid. Many are concerned that we are becoming too politically correct. Recently, a member in a forum to which I belong responded to new anti-bullying legislation as "nanny state gobbledygook," adding that this was yet "one more of these types of state-imposed, declining-return, bureaucratic laws that forces us into yet more red tape." Clearly, not everyone believes that there is a need for additional legislative restrictions on disrespectful behavior in the workplace.

The movement toward a more conservative and restricted workplace stands in stark contradiction to the increased freedoms that the same legislators and courts afford to citizens of society at large. At the newspaper stand right outside your office building you will find an abundant display of scantily dressed women and sexually explicit front-page headlines; however, once you walk through the door of your workplace just steps away, you are required to abide by a completely different set of rules.

To further complicate the matter, the lines between what is okay and what is not okay are moving at different paces across industries.

Some industries have traditionally relied on a rougher style, one that would nowadays be considered as harassment and certainly uncivil.

In that spirited session with the overall-clad workmen I described earlier in the book, I was the only woman in a room jam-packed with thirty men who made their living working the power lines that supplied electricity to the area. In a mix of lively bantering and discussion of serious matters, I did my best to challenge their thinking and open their minds to realize (grudgingly) that the landscape had changed and that nowadays employers had to do things differently, which would require each and every one of them to change as well.

They were appalled at my assertion that, no, they did not have the right to post pictures of nude women inside their lockers (they seemed to forget that the company had recently made that rule quite clear). They tried arguing that it was perfectly fine to have those same pictures openly displayed on the back window of their cars ("That's my personal property!") in the company's parking lot. It didn't help much that the union president sat right near me, openly endorsing my message; these folks were insistent on what they perceived as their rights. My only consolation was that in the end-of-session evaluations an overwhelming majority indicated that they had learned—and would apply—valuable new ideas.

In some industries, the trend toward a more respectful environment is happening at an accelerated pace. Some organizations in the construction business, for example, are discovering that younger people who enter the workforce are no longer willing to contend with "old boys" practices. They see no redeeming value in the old ways of doing things, where you earn your stripes by copying your boss's rough, sometimes bully-style, habits. They expect to be treated with respect and to operate within a dignity-based workplace context. If they don't get that, they pack up their talent and move on to an organization that will provide what they are looking for. Therefore, future-oriented firms in this sector are moving rapidly toward creating a more civil culture. They fear losing their competitive edge if they do not do so.

In your role as a leader, the challenge is to determine where the line of civility falls in your particular work environment, and how you can help your people avoid crossing it. This is no small feat; what may be a perfectly acceptable behavior in your organization might be a complete no-no in the business next door, or even for the team on the other side of the wall.

RAISE THE BANNER: A CIVILITY LITMUS TEST

With banner flip-flapping,
Once more you'll ride high!
Ready for anything under the sky.
Ready because you're that kind of guy!
—Dr. Seuss, Oh, the Places You'll Go!

Here's a piece of good news: I've devised a simple, industrial-strength "line test" that will help you determine whether that invisible line that separates civility from incivility has been crossed. Similar to a litmus test, it's a diagnostic assessment of sorts, a tool that you run in your mind to assess situations quickly and come to a fast and relatively accurate conclusion. When certain behavior does not meet the bar set by your line test, it means that you as a leader have to do something about it. It is your responsibility to take action. This tool is flexible enough to be useful to you in any organization you might work in, even as times and sensibilities keep changing.

Here's how this line test works:

Step 1

Whenever a situation doesn't feel right (in that special canary way), imagine in your mind's eye that the words that were just spoken are placed on an attractive, huge and colorful banner. Or, alternatively, the behavior that caused your canary to awaken was captured on looping videotape that continuously replays it. So, the banner might say, for example, "That's not my job to do, and besides, can't you see that I'm already busy?!" Or the looping video might show an employee talking to another, who visibly rolls her eyes and makes a dismissive hissing sound in response to what he's saying.

Step 2

Now, imagine that the fancy banner or looping video is hung right above the front entrance to your establishment, in plain view, so that each and every person who enters your premises can see it and get a vivid sense of the kinds of behaviors that occur in your organization behind closed doors. Your clients will all be able to see it. Talented candidates will see it when they come for their first job interview. Visiting dignitaries who travel from afar to learn about your organization's achievements will see it. Potential investors will get a sense of what your company is really all about. Employees' family members will see it when they come to visit on Family Day.

If you are comfortable with the world seeing the banner or video, then the behavior that caused you concern in the first place is perfectly all right. However, if you cringe at the thought of the world forming an impression of your organization based on that banner or video, then the line between civility and incivility, professionalism and unprofessionalism, has been crossed. The behavior compromises the brand and is corrosive to the organizational culture. Your litmus test has determined that the conduct in some way violates the sensibilities of your organization and team as they are at this particular time.

This strategy is, therefore, called Raise the Banner. When a behavior does not pass the litmus test, it is your job as a leader to Raise the Banner and help people change the manner in which they are behaving.

Raise the Banner follows in the footsteps of the two previous strategies: First, you need to commit to minding the windows. Then, in situations where your canary alerts you that something is wrong, you need to trust your canary. Once you do that, you might still need to unpack that gut feeling and attach a more rational logic to it. From there you proceed to perform a quick litmus test to determine whether or not this behavior is acceptable in the context of the company and the times, which you do by Raising the Banner.

Bannerese for All

The best way to boost civility is to involve everyone in making it happen. Once people get emotionally connected to the importance of this issue, they are more motivated to act as responsible organizational citizens. And the more such committed citizens you have (especially if they are able to articulate *why* they are doing what they are doing and *how* they are going about it), the better. Suddenly, before you know it, you have a strong civility culture.

To this end, I encourage you to teach your staff a new language—Bannerese. That is, equip the team (or even the entire organization) with a common language to use around the concept of civility. Share the banner litmus test with them and develop ongoing dialogue about civil behaviors that everyone on the team aspires to and would like to promote. The banner metaphor is easy to grasp and removes much of the confusion about those ever-shifting lines. In our training sessions, we have found that people immediately grasp this image and gravitate toward it. They quickly understand that even though some behaviors may feel natural and acceptable in the context of a team's specific culture, once you bare them for the world to see, they may not actually pass muster.

After you familiarize everyone with the banner notion, encourage people to use it as shorthand to help each other behave in a civil fashion. "Watch the banner!" is a simple, innocent phrase that serves as a supportive and friendly reminder to a person that his or her behavior is close to, or has already crossed, the line of acceptability.

Initiate ongoing discussion in your team about "lines" and "banners"—why they are important, what needs to happen to uphold them and how people can support each other in raising the banner.

Once you teach everyone to speak Bannerese, you too can correct behaviors using a shorthand reference to the banner. It's a concise and highly effective way of communicating a constructive message without laying blame or placing someone in an uncomfortable position. The image of the banner is a simple reminder that everyone in this environment aspires to contribute to a culture that everyone can be proud of.

IMPLEMENTATION CLINIC

Your Ancestors' Gift

Your inner canary is your built-in incivility detector, developed and fine-tuned over thousands of years. This gut-reaction gauge alerts you to the presence of a problem and indicates that you as a leader are required to take action to restore civility and respect.

Not all canaries are created equal. To understand yours, think back to a workplace situation where your gut told you that a situation you observed, participated in or were told about was uncivil, disrespectful or otherwise violated a person's dignity.

1. Did you experience a physical sensation or discomfort when this occurred? If so, what was the specific nature of the sensation?

2. Did you act on your sense that something wasn't right?

3. If you took no specific action, what were the barriers (within yourself or external)?

4. If you took no action, what happened to your original sense of discomfort over time?

5. In hindsight, what (in specific terms) would you have done differently? Why?

6. What will help you act on the alert from your canary more decisively next time?

7. What might hinder such action next time?

IMPLEMENTATION CLINIC

Raise the Banner:
"If It Can't Be on the Banner, Change the Manner!"

The line between acceptable and unacceptable behavior is shifting at an ever-accelerating pace. When the line is crossed, it damages the company brand and corrodes organizational and team cultures.

In your role as a leader, you are entrusted with safeguarding that line of civility.

When you (or your inner canary) encounter questionable conduct, run this line test, or litmus test, quickly through your mind: Imagine a banner or video depicting that behavior hanging above the company's front door, for the world to see. If you cringe at the thought of displaying this behavior publicly, it means that the behavior has crossed the line of acceptability.

Now, it's your job as a leader to tend to it.

Reflect on the following:

- Consider a situation where your canary got activated and you did not intervene because you were unsure of whether or not the behavior was wrong.

  - What prevented you from reacting?

  - Had you run the line test at that moment, what would you have discovered?

  - How would that have changed the situation and its outcome?

(continued)

- If you share the line test with your staff and teach them to speak Bannerese, what benefits might that offer? What difference will it make?

- Would it make sense for you to share the line test with your staff and, if so, why?

- How (specifically) would you go about doing so?

* * *

9

TOOLS OF THE TRADE
SCREWDRIVERS AT YOUR DISPOSAL

....

With your head full of brains and your shoes full of feet,
You're too smart to go down any not-so-good street.
—Dr. Seuss, Oh, the Places You'll Go!

GETTING THE SUPPORT YOU NEED

Every respect-related situation is different from the one before it and from the one that will follow. Even the most minor of differences in any element of a situation will require a different analysis, and a somewhat different solution.

And yet, most managers continue to apply the same set of solutions that they are most comfortable with over and over, even though the results may be utterly ineffective. I have seen managers who are great believers in mediation, so they attempt to change people's uncivil behavior though coaching, even when performance management for one of the players would have been the right solution. Other times, a manager who may have been burned by a past harassment situation that backfired because it was not reported feels compelled to take a heavy and formal approach for fear of future problems, even though a lighter and informal approach would have yielded better results.

Let's use the analogy of screws and screwdrivers. The respect-related problems you encounter are analogous to screws, where each screw head is different: you have Robertson, Phillips, slotted or hex, to name a few, and each requires the complementary screwdriver to be removed effectively. The range of strategies available to you as a manager to deal with any given situation is as wide as the range of available screwdrivers, and to be effective you need to apply the right strategy or strategies to the situation at hand. The problem is that, if you are like most leaders, you might love your Phillips screwdriver and trust in your ability to use it well, and you will tend to think that every screw you encounter has a Phillips head. You will pry your Phillips screwdriver into that screw again and again, despite clear evidence that the screw is not relenting at all. And if you love your Robertson screwdriver, well then, every screw seems like a Robertson.

The key to any intervention to address a specific incivility challenge successfully is to use the right screwdriver. Take a Phillips to a Phillips head, a Robertson to a Robertson head, a slot screwdriver to a straight-head screw.

Up until now we have explored the many ways that you can diagnose situations. You learned how to trust your inner canary and how to identify when behavior does not belong on the banner above your company's front door. From here onward, we will focus on understanding what metaphorical screwdrivers are available to you, the unique features of each, their advantages and disadvantages, and when you should use each tool—and in what combinations.

Let's begin by reviewing the broader options that you can pursue: what you can do, and the resources you can and should access to assist you in preventing or dealing with incivility.

Consult Your Own Manager

Chances are that your manager has had some valuable experience and may have accumulated some wisdom along his or her path. At times, he or she may possess institutional knowledge and history of which you may not be aware. For these reasons alone, it is a good idea always to ask yourself whether you should consult your manager before, during, or after you are dealing with an incivility-related situation.

But there's another advantage to consulting your manager that you may not have considered. When you begin to address incivility in a more systematic fashion, things can get messy. People who may have become used to behaving as they wish without any accountability can react in strong ways to your attempts to change the landscape. For example, when you begin to address the behavior of a chronically uncivil staff member, this person might launch a grievance accusing you of bullying. Before you know it, you might be in big trouble. Accessing your manager's insight and guidance from the very beginning might prove invaluable. Having your manager in the know will help protect your reputation and standing if things go south.

Consult a Trusted Colleague

A colleague whose opinions you respect is a huge asset. With such a colleague you can share your true hesitations, concerns and even fears in ways that you may not feel as comfortable doing with your own manager. Your colleague will keep your affairs in confidence, and will be there for you in moments of confusion, self-doubt or frustration. Whenever possible, choose a person who feels comfortable in challenging you and helping you stretch your envelope so that you can go into places that might feel uncomfortable initially, but will help you grow as a leader.

Consult Human Resources or Employee Relations

In some organizations, the human resources and/or employee relations departments expect you to access their expertise as frequently as you need to and on any matter where you deem it necessary to do so. They are able and willing to help in preventing problems or dealing with them once they occur, and see their role as supporting you on your journey as a leader. In other organizations, managers are expected to solve problems on their own, and escalate them to human resources or employee relations only when the issues reach a certain severity level.

If you trust your human resources department and the expertise that they bring to the table, then go ahead and leverage this resource as much as possible. A solid, knowledgeable and commonsensical human resources partner at your side can save you from falling into unnecessary traps and provide you with step-by-step solutions to resolving complex situations.

Access Your Internal Organizational Development Experts

If you are lucky enough to work in an organization that has an organizational development department (or organizational effectiveness experts) that is not already bogged down by many other requests, this might be an excellent resource to help you transform your team or division into a civil, high-performing unit. Accessing this type of expertise is particularly useful when the work unit suffers from chronic incivility.

Members of this department will take a systematic approach that brings into consideration factors in the organizational milieu as well as the concrete challenges you face on the ground, and will offer the best solutions accordingly. You can expect them to implement surveys, perform interviews with select people, suggest changes to work processes or roles if these play a part in agitating relationships, help you create team norms and more.

Engage External Consultants

External consultants can offer a range of services, including the type of services that an internal organizational development department might be able to offer in-house.

A good organizational consultant will conduct a thorough needs assessment to understand the challenges you face and offer solutions that are tailored to your unique situation. Avoid service providers that offer canned solutions because these may not sufficiently fit your needs. At best, this will not be a good use of your organizational funds. At worst, it will exacerbate the problem that you are already having and erode your credibility as a leader.

Access Training or Coaching for Yourself

Leadership is a continuous journey of growth, discovery, trial and error. The best way to learn and grow as a leader is by learning from your own experience, successes and failures. But as you probably already know, it is exceedingly difficult to find that precious time for reflection. In the midst of deadlines and urgent demands, time to quiet down and consider your experiences and what they mean is in extremely short supply.

A good coach will ask you tough questions about your counterproductive beliefs, behaviors and blind spots, and help ensure that you are walking the talk. He or she will assist you in developing a concrete vision for team civility and in being accountable for your goals. The coaching sessions will offer an invaluable opportunity to find refuge from the bustling world of performing and enter into the saner world of thinking and reflecting, from which you can then emerge into meaningful action to boost team civility.

You can also boost your skill level for dealing with incivility by pursuing training. If your organization offers in-house respect training for leaders, you will have the luxury of sitting with a group of colleagues who all work in the same environment and share similar challenges. Learning together and acquiring the same tools at the same time will enable you to learn from your colleagues' experiences and insights and, over time, (hopefully) implement similar strategies across the board.

If your organization does not provide civility training on-site (at the time of writing, few do), explore whether there are public workshops that you can attend. Make sure that the course for which you register is offered by a reputable organization and that the content is suitable to your needs. Some training organizations offer a very legalistic approach to this type of training, which may or may not be useful to your context and personal learning needs.

WHAT TO DO: ACTION PLANNING CRITERIA

Chances are that you have other matters on your agenda besides boosting civility on your team. There is so much to do, on all fronts, and dealing with incivility can be complex. You might find yourself feeling discouraged or even overwhelmed. And we humans tend to procrastinate when we feel discouraged. As a result, nothing gets done.

You will need to be thoughtful about where you spend your effort and time. Use the following criteria to determine what you should focus on, when and how.

Which actions, once implemented, will be most aligned with your personal legacy and the way in which you want to be remembered many years from now?

This question will help you go to the heart of what really matters to you as a person and leader. It connects you with your inner conviction and sense of meaning. For example, if you want to be remembered as compassionate, then the actions you should focus on first will revolve around ensuring that a team member who is marginalized gets included more. Find a time and place where you can get still and reflect deeply on this question. When the answers bubble up from within, trust them and use them as a compass to guide your broader decision-making process.

Which ideas are low-hanging fruit?

The term "low-hanging fruit" refers to ideas and strategies that are easy to implement within a relatively short time. Review the ideas offered in this and other chapters, as well as ideas that you have considered or even tried, and assess which ones you can apply with little effort and are worthwhile doing.

Which action(s) are urgent and must be taken immediately?

Some items simply cannot wait, and you have to take action immediately. If, for example, incivility levels have reached the harassment or bullying threshold, do not wait until you take care of other business. The time to act is now, decisively and visibly. The same is true if your customers (or clients, or patients) are complaining about specific people or behaviors. Here, too, action should be taken immediately.

Which actions will offer the most visibility?

When things have been a certain way for a long time, people may not register the changes you are making. Therefore, when you embark on an effort to change things in a meaningful fashion, you will need to consider bringing a certain level of visibility to the action that you plan to take. For example, if you decide to actively take on chronic offenders, consider announcing in a big way that change is coming and the rationale behind it—in a team meeting, an email sent to all team members, a hard-copy memo, one-one-one interactions or all of the above.

Which action is important but not urgent?

Stephen Covey, in *The 7 Habits of Highly Effective People*, noted the importance of being proactive by tending well in advance to matters that are important but not urgent—those issues that are crucial for long-term success but tend to be pushed aside by seemingly more pressing priorities. For example, having a clear process for orienting a new team member to the civility norms the team has agreed upon in its team-norms document is an important-not-urgent matter; but if you don't put such a process in place, a new team member might behave in a way that violates the team norms and tarnish their own reputation from the get-go. Don't neglect the important-not-urgent items, because if you don't take action on these types of matters, they have a peculiar way of becoming urgent.

Which action, once taken, will provide the best return on investment (ROI)?

ROI can be measured in different ways, such as the monetary, time, effort or other resources necessary to bring the initiative to life relative to the benefits gained. Some initiatives may not require any monetary investment but will yield great results. For example, you could appoint a few team members to identify fun games and activities to celebrate civility at your quarterly all-staff meetings. Not only will you end up with a team that is more aware of civility, but your "fun committee" will also become change agents and civility champions.

Which action, once taken, will create a meaningful ripple effect?

Some actions you take will snowball faster than others. It is not always possible to predict at the outset which activities will have a more wide-ranging ripple effect, but you certainly can attempt to make such predictions. For example, will establishing team norms (which we will discuss in detail in chapter 12 when we review prevention touchstones) trigger more lasting results than influencing a highly respected and popular team member into becoming a champion of change?

REFLECT ON the unique circumstances you face, and as you consider some of the above criteria, it may become clear to you where to begin and where to go from there. As you go through this consideration process, you may want to seek input from the sources discussed earlier in this chapter, such as your manager, a trusted colleague, an outside consultant or your internal organizational development experts.

Now that you've discovered how to adopt the broken-window philosophy and how to identify when the line of civility is crossed, using the wisdom of your own canary and that litmus test, the rest of the book will focus on an array of metaphorical screwdrivers, tools that you can use to address any incivility-related situation appropriately, confidently and competently.

IMPLEMENTATION CLINIC

Using the Right Screwdriver

In the same way that every screw requires the use of a screwdriver that fits it, so too do your interventions on the incivility front require you to use the right approach, at the right time, with the right people, in the right way. To help you arrive at best results, consider consulting or accessing expertise from—

- your manager
- a trusted colleague
- human resources or employee relations
- internal organizational development experts
- external consultants
- training or coaching for yourself

The universe of actions you can take is endless. You will need to decide how best to expend your time and efforts. To arrive at the best plan, ask yourself, which action or actions—

- are most aligned with your personal legacy?
- are low-hanging fruit?
- are urgent and must be taken immediately?
- will offer most visibility?
- are important but not urgent?
- will provide the best return on investment (ROI)?
- will create a meaningful ripple effect?

10

PROVIDE CORRECTIVE FEEDBACK

FOLLOW THE S-B-D METHOD

....

So be sure when you step,
Step with care and great tact
And remember that life's
A Great Balancing Act.
—Dr. Seuss, Oh, the Places You'll Go!

IN PRAISE OF A SOLID STRUCTURE

My guess is that, like most leaders, addressing bad behavior is not on your list of favorite things to do. You probably feel that there are numerous better ways for you to use your talent and time. However, correcting uncivil behavior is as important as many of the other things you do as a leader, and leaving it unchallenged leads to serious problems for the business down the road. Like the sweepers in the game of curling that we spoke of earlier in the book, your job is to clear the way so that team and organizational objectives can be achieved.

Most issues related to uncivil behavior are resolvable with little effort, if this effort is undertaken early on. The right words at the right time can go a long way. However, you might find yourself avoiding having those conversations, even though you know full well that they need to happen sooner rather than later. Even when your canary has spoken, and even after you've committed to fixing broken windows, you still might find yourself in that no-man's land of procrastination.

Paradoxically, you might be procrastinating because you aspire to be a kind and decent human being, and addressing uncivil behavior translates in your subconscious mind into "I must be a bad person if I inflict this negative feedback on a fellow human being." Your sense of inner decency and unwillingness to impose hardship on another person may lead to avoidance. You will ignore things as they get worse, telling yourself that the problem will get resolved on its own or that it's really not that serious, or you will persuade yourself that you have more pressing priorities. Meanwhile, things on the ground might be getting worse. Rather than resolving the problem, your procrastination exacerbates matters.

Much of your avoidance and anxiety can be prevented by having a solid framework that you can rely on, the kind of framework that allows you to deal with uncivil behavior confidently and effectively, and that can melt problems away if employed early enough. The S-B-D feedback method will help you navigate any conversation about problem behavior in a supportive, firm and fair manner. Using this approach will help turn things around. And in those moments when you don't know what to do and how to respond, you can hold onto this structure for dear life.

TWO USEFUL STRATEGIES TO INCREASE THE CHANCES OF SUCCESS

When you address an incivility issue with someone, there's a good chance that he or she will get defensive. So before we get down to the specifics of the S-B-D approach, let's look at two strategies that will significantly increase the chances that your feedback will be received with more openness and less defensiveness than it otherwise would. When defensiveness is low and openness is high, the likelihood of a behavior change is exponentially higher. And, after all, that is exactly what you are hoping to achieve.

Strategy 1: Manage Your Body Language

The higher the congruence between your verbal and nonverbal messages, the lower the chances are that the person receiving the feedback will misinterpret the message or become defensive. Don't fall into the trap of saying one thing with your words while communicating something entirely different with your tone, facial expressions or other body language.

All communication channels should convey calm and neutrality. Leave your emotions out of the picture. Remind yourself that you are correcting behavior because you have committed to creating a civil work environment and that it is imperative that your personal feelings and judgments stay out of the picture.

Here are some areas of your body to monitor before you provide feedback and while you are doing it:

- A relaxed jaw, biting surfaces of the teeth slightly separated
- Calm and open expression, including a relaxed forehead
- Breathing from your diaphragm
- Relaxed shoulders

Strategy 2: Own Your Contribution

Let's face it: in many instances where you need to address workplace incivility, your own conduct has probably in some way contributed to the current state of affairs. Your role may have been minimal but, still, it played a part. Here are some common examples where you may have inadvertently contributed to the problem:

- You modeled uncivil behavior.
- You didn't articulate the expectations clearly enough to begin with.
- You procrastinated instead of acting earlier.
- You joined in on the behavior in some way.
- You made no reference to your concerns as part of the performance appraisal process.
- You permitted other staff to get away with similar behaviors.

Owning the ways in which your own behavior has contributed to the problem at hand will go a long way to ensuring positive results. (Doing so is especially important when dealing with chronically uncivil individuals, an issue we will discuss in chapter 13.) If you don't own your side of things, the people whose behavior you are addressing will naturally get defensive. After all, why shouldn't they? From their perspective, they feel that they are treated unfairly. In their mind, you are blaming them for something for which you, too, are partially responsible. And when their mind goes to these places, their hearing is shut down. The fight-or-flight response will kick in and with it the inability to be logical or hear what you are saying. The conversation is now doomed.

Here's how owning your contribution might sound:

"I want to acknowledge my own part in this situation. I have observed these behaviors previously and not intervened. In doing so, I gave the impression that it was okay to engage in this type of behavior. I take full

responsibility for not letting you know that in fact this was not acceptable and apologize for not being clearer, earlier."

THE S-B-D FEEDBACK METHOD, STEP-BY-STEP

- *"As you know, we've committed to civility. Foul language doesn't fit, so let's cut it out."*

- *"Ruena, I'd like to speak with you for a moment. At Best Bakers we expect mutual respect, even when we are busy or disagree with each other. In our team meeting just now, you arrived late without advance notice. We couldn't start without you because you had the computer with all the data. Then, as Jack was presenting, you gave a loud sigh and said that you had more pressing things to do right now than to sit in this meeting. I'm concerned about this behavior because it doesn't fit with our commitment to a respectful work culture. I ask that you arrive on time to meetings or make appropriate arrangements if you know you will be late. Equally as important, please avoid making dismissive comments or gestures. If you disagree with a person or an idea, state your reservations in a professional way, directly and using constructive language."*

What is the common denominator between these two statements? Both are examples of the S-B-D three-step feedback method in action. Both examples use the exact same steps, with a different flavor and length. Once you learn how to construct this feedback, you will be able to adapt the method to any situation in which you wish to provide corrective civility-related feedback. You'll be able to adapt it to different circumstances as feedback one-on-one or in the presence of several people, making it long or short, and delivering it in either a formal or informal tone.

In instances where you need to use the S-B-D process on the spot, right in the moment, using it in very short form is often the best route to go. Other times, you will use it as part of a conversation that takes place after the fact and in private, and here you may want to go into more detail. Regardless, use it as a chassis upon which to construct your own message, leveraging your own strengths and unique style.

Setting the Stage with an Introductory Comment

Before delving into the actual feedback you want to deliver, make an introductory comment. The purpose of such comments is to frame the context, clarify your purpose and increase the chances of opening the other person's mind to being receptive to what you have to say. Below you will find examples of such opening comments:

- *"Nora, you've told me how you wanted to excel and find more opportunities within the company. I'd like to take a few minutes to talk about something that could be an obstacle in your way."*

- *"Nick, when I took on management of the team three months ago, I shared that my mission was to help us serve our clients better by building a strong culture of mutual respect. I wanted to share with you a concern I have in this regard."*

- *"Paula, do you have a moment? I want to bring to your attention something that you may not be aware of. My purpose is to help you and help make our team better."*

Of course, an introductory comment is not always necessary. When the feedback is short, you may want to get right to the point and not use an introductory comment.

At the heart of the S-B-D method lie the following steps:

Table 7: The S-B-D Method

Step 1	**S** = State the expectation (= the standard that people are expected to follow)
Step 2	**B** = Behavior (= the current problem behavior)
Step 3	**D** = Desired behavior (= what the person should do differently)

(A little confession: it is not entirely a coincidence that the S-B-D acronym is identical to the initials of my name, Sharone Bar-David. I hope that in the moment when you need to provide this feedback, you will imagine me as a supportive coach perched on your shoulder and whispering to you, "You can do it, you can do it!")

Step 1: **S** = State the Expectation

In this step, you outline the broad expectation that defines how everyone in the organization (or division, or team or unit) should conduct himself or herself in the workplace. Here, you refer to overarching values, the culture you aspire to or behavioral expectations. You can describe the expectation in big-picture terms (as in the first two examples below), or in terms that relate directly to the issue itself (as in the second two examples).

Here's how this segment might sound:

- *"Here at Broad-View we aspire to an inclusive and accepting culture."*

- *"In our division, everyone's opinions and skills count."*

- "Being able to innovate is vital to what our team does. It's crucial that people feel free to express ideas without being worried about being ridiculed or mocked."

- "In sales, we maintain our calm, especially when the heat is on and everyone is stretched to the limit."

The person with whom you are speaking might not be fully aware of the broader expectation, so beginning with the bigger picture raises their awareness of policies, values and norms that everyone is expected to follow on the organizational or team level. Other times, it reminds them of what they already know but may not be practicing.

Notice that these examples express an expectation that applies to everyone. This is not about you as a specific manager or about the specific employee. Rather, it is what is required of everyone, across the board. This angle makes the message less personal and, therefore, less blaming. It also implicitly explains the rationale for your insistence on making change happen. In addition, describing the expected standard makes it easier to demonstrate in the next part of the message how exactly the person's behavior falls short of the expectation.

Step 2: **B** = Behavior

In this stage of offering feedback, you describe the uncivil behavior in question. You do this because the person needs to understand the exact nature of your concern. While you (or the person who complained to you) are very aware of the problematic nature of the behavior, the person with whom you are speaking may not be aware of his or her conduct, or may not realize the impact it has on others. An excellent example of this is eye-rolling: Some people automatically roll their eyes when they are frustrated with someone, with absolutely no awareness that they are doing so. And they certainly are not aware of the negative impact this behavior has on those who are the subject of it.

Use video-camera language to describe the behavior. That is, depict it as if it had been captured on a video camera, without the interpretation or emotional inflection of a narrator. A video camera takes images of body gestures, facial expressions, words and tone, but it does not capture diagnoses, conclusions or abstractions. Be as precise as possible in your description and whenever possible quote some or all of the actual words that the person said, or at least paraphrase them to the best of your ability. For example, don't say, "Shooting down Raoul's idea was rude and humiliating," which sounds judgmental and accusatory and interprets the emotional effect on Raoul. Instead say, "When Raoul suggested that we use a different format in our reporting, you said in front of three other colleagues that Raoul had no clue what he was saying."

Here's a sample list of words that a video camera would not capture (and that you therefore should avoid using when you describe the behavior itself):

- Angry
- Hostile
- Rude
- Intrusive
- Uncooperative
- Negative
- Disruptive
- Inconsiderate

Even the most advanced video camera would be incapable of capturing these terms in the behavior itself. They represent a conclusion that the manager might arrive at by synthesizing a number of behaviors and lumping them under one word. For example, "angry" is a synthesis of observable behaviors such a raised voice, finger pointing, reddened face, hand waving or very slow speech. If you use synthesizing terms instead of describing the behavior in video-speak, the person will not get a clear picture of what exactly you see as the problem. As a result, he or she will not know what they need to change.

Furthermore, when you use words such as "rude," "angry," "hostile," "intrusive" and the like, you will invariably trigger a negative reaction in the person at whom these terms are directed. He or she will naturally experience your characterization of their behavior as an unfair indictment and feel compelled to refute. I therefore highly recommend avoiding general terms; they are both unfair and unhelpful.

If your mind takes you to words such as "rude" or "hostile," you'll need to unpack these words to arrive at the behaviors that led you to using them in the first place. A great way to do this is by asking yourself:

- What did I see or hear that led me to conclude that the person was hostile?
- What would a video camera capture that would lead a viewer to conclude that the person in the video was being rude?

Given all the above, the behavior segment of the S-B-D feedback might sound like this:

"I've been made aware that for the past several days, you've been telling people that you're in a bad mood and that they shouldn't mess with you. I understand that when Maya approached you yesterday with a question regarding the operating instructions for the new heaters, you asked her in the presence of three other colleagues whether she had not heard that you don't want to be bothered with stupid things."

As you can see, the manager in this case took the time to outline the behavior and used actual quotes. True, the person receiving this feedback will in all likelihood not feel all warm and fuzzy when hearing it, but at least it is an objective description of what happened, not an unfair accusation.

And here's how the manager could have got it all wrong and led the person on the receiving end to become angry, upset and likely hostile (as you read this, ask yourself which words you think would lead to undesirable results):

"I've been made aware that for the past several days, you've been in a crabby mood and broadcasting don't-mess-with-me warnings to pretty much everyone around you. To add insult to injury, you humiliated Maya in front of a bunch of colleagues by calling her stupid and brushing her off like she didn't know what she was doing."

You probably were able to identify all or some of the problematic language: *crabby, broadcasting, pretty much everyone, insult to injury, humiliated, bunch of colleagues, brushing her off like she didn't know what she was doing*. It is highly unlikely that using this approach will encourage the person on the receiving end to take ownership for his or her behavior and to move forward productively.

As you read all this, you might be thinking, "But, Sharone, what about the situations where someone complains to me about uncivil behavior that I have not observed with my own eyes? How can I use video-speak under those circumstances without falling into problematic language?"

Great question. When someone brings to your attention a situation that you did not personally observe, your first step will be to obtain from that person a detailed description of the problem in—you guessed it!—video-camera language. This step is crucial because, without it, you will not be able to offer the uncivil person a helpful and fair description of the behavior when you speak with them about the need to change. To elicit useful descriptions from the complainant, use the same line of inquiry suggested above: "What did you see or hear that led you to say that Jocelyn was dismissive?" Once you obtain concrete descriptions, you can then proceed successfully in the same way that the manager in the example above did.

Augmenting the Message to Decrease Defensiveness

There are two elements you can add to the S-B-D method to help deepen the message as well as to preempt unnecessary upset. Both fit nicely within the "behavior" segment of the S-B-D method, though you can use them later on as well.

Augmentation No. 1: Describe the impact of the behavior

Include a description of the impact that the behavior has had on others or on the environment. If there has been no impact yet, you could describe the impact it might potentially have. Here you can digress from using video-speak and include more of those conclusion-type words that I recommended you avoid when describing the behavior itself.

Here's how including the impact might sound:

- *"Using this type of language discounts other people's experience and skills."*

- *"This type of comment can create rifts between team members."*

- *"This behavior is disruptive to others and creates a negative environment."*

- *"This type of behavior can have the effect of . . ."*

Augmentation No. 2: Assign benevolence—offer the benefit of the doubt

Most people are not intentionally uncivil. They do not mean to harm, upset or offend even though their actions might have exactly that effect. The purpose of you providing corrective feedback is to get people to change, and the chances of that happening are much higher if you let them know that you understand that their intentions were not malevolent.

Therefore, whenever possible, add to your message an element that coveys exactly that: I know you did not intend anything bad. Here's how it might sound:

- "I'm sure that your intention was to be helpful, and not necessarily to be critical."
- "I realize that anyone can say or do things in the moment that one would not do or say if one had a chance to think a little more."
- "You're a great team player, and I know that excluding someone is not something that you would do intentionally."
- "My sense is that you did not intend to belittle, offend or upset."

Step 3: **D** = Desired Behavior

Relaying an expectation and informing a person that his or her behavior falls short of meeting that expectation is only half the job. Your role as a wise and fair leader is to show the way by sharing with the person the desired behavior that you expect to see. This is where the "D" step comes in: desired behavior (or desired change).

The main objective for this step in providing feedback is to provide the person with a tangible sense of a preferred mode of conduct. A blueprint, if you will. Outline the behavior that you expect to see in future. Choose whether to use concrete behavioral terms (always a great thing to do) or to provide general direction without the specifics.

The Desired Behavior step might look like this:

- "I ask that you not use your mobile device during meetings. If ever there are circumstances where you know you will absolutely need to use it, please let other meeting participants know about this at the outset and seek their input as to the best way to handle this without disrupting the meeting."

- "In future, please be inclusive, even with people who are not necessarily in your close circle."

PULLING THE S-B-D FEEDBACK TOGETHER

The S-B-D method is a flexible structure that you can apply in whatever way feels comfortable to you. The two examples used in the opening part of this segment ("The S-B-D Feedback Method Step-by-Step") highlighted two very different ways of using the method. You will decide, based on your judgment, whether to use a longer approach or a short one, a serious tone or a lighter one. Here are some quick and dirty guidelines:

1. When responding in public, keep it short.
2. When the person is new to the organization (or country), use a more educational approach—longer and detailed, with special attention to the expectations part.
3. When the person already knows what's expected but had a little slip, a short reminder will do.
4. When the issue is really important, provide details and consider emphasizing the desired behavior.
5. When the feedback is provided in the midst of other activities, be brief.

The Dialogue Piece

When appropriate, it is important to create a space for hearing the employee's perspective. In some cases you might even choose to have that broader dialogue right after you describe the problem behavior, and only after that part of the conversation to add the piece about the desired and expected behavior going forward. This is most useful when you did not observe the problematic behavior with your own eyes or when the situation is complex and you need to be clearer about what exactly you should say about the desired behavior. Inserting the dialogue piece midway is also suitable in situations where the feedback is provided in a longer fashion, as part of a more reflective conversation rather than a one-sided or brief comment.

As part of the dialogue, the employee might acknowledge the behavior and express an intention to avoid it in the future, possibly even expressing regret. Other times, the conversation that develops might focus on planning together how to bring about change, possibly with some coaching from you.

And sometimes, as life would have it, things will get more complicated. You will encounter objections, defensiveness and strong emotions. In these instances, you'll need to listen carefully, acknowledge respectfully—and stick to your resolve and sense of purpose while doing so. Regardless of any protest you may encounter, you as the leader have the right and obligation to require that people behave in a civil and professional manner on the job.

Table 8: Checklist: Preparing for the Meeting

> Here are questions to consider as part of your planning for any conversation with an employee regarding problem performance:
> - What do you need to have on hand for the meeting?
> - Should you consult with anyone prior to the meeting? If so, whom?
> - Where will be the optimal place to hold the meeting? What time of day is best?
> - Does anyone else need to attend the meeting? Who?
> - When will you invite the employee and what precisely will you say?
> - What are your general objectives for the meeting?
> - What is a nonnegotiable outcome for the meeting, your bottom line?
> - How will you begin the conversation?
> - What do you need to understand or learn during the meeting?
> - How will you ensure that the conversation remains on track?

IMPLEMENTATION CLINIC

Do an S-B-D

When you need to provide corrective feedback, relying on a solid structure will help you deliver your message confidently, succinctly and without triggering defensive reactions within the other person. The S-B-D method provides you with this structure:

S = State the expectation.
B = Describe the problem behavior.
D = Outline the desired behavior (or change).

Consider also:

1. Setting a positive tone with an introductory comment.

2. Extending the benefit of the doubt; assume and express that they had benevolent intention.

3. Describing the impact (or potential impact) of the behavior.

4. Admitting to your part in the problem.

5. Sticking to observable behavior.

6. Opening space for dialogue.

7. Controlling your body language throughout the conversation.

REFLECTION

1. What do you experience as the most challenging element of providing corrective feedback? Why?

2. What is your greatest strength in providing such feedback?

3. What is one thing you need to get better at in order to be truly effective in helping change someone's behavior?

4. How can you use the ideas in this chapter to deliver corrective feedback in the best possible way?

* * *

11

GO PUBLIC
HANDLING SITUATIONS THAT
HAPPEN IN FRONT OF OTHERS

• •

And IF you go in, should you turn left or right . . .
Or right-and-three-quarters? Or, maybe, not quite?
—Dr. Seuss, Oh, the Places You'll Go!

THE IMPERATIVE TO RESPOND IN PUBLIC

Rushing between meetings, you drop by the coffee machine, situated within hearing range of workspaces. There are five people standing by the coffee machine. Two of these people report directly to you, one works in another department, the fourth person seems vaguely familiar and the fifth is dressed in business attire, carrying a briefcase and seems quite formal.

A minute into it, you overhear the staff member who works in another department questioning the work of a coworker who is not present in a condescending and snippy tone. Although it is reasonable for this employee to question what the other did, your inner canary immediately alerts you that a line has been crossed in the way that the message was delivered. You run the banner litmus test in your mind ("How would this behavior look if it played on a video above our front entrance?" Hmm, not good.) You realize that you need to take action to fix this "broken window" of uncivil behavior. You are acutely aware that you are wearing a badge that identifies you as a manager and that at least one of the people present is an outsider.

What should you do in this situation?

As you consider this (challenging) situation, your first instinct might be to take this person aside and tell him or her that the behavior was inappropriate. And maybe you'd even decide that later on you will also speak with the two people who report to you, who were also there when it happened.

If that was your response, you are certainly acting in congruence with the golden rule of good management: Praise publicly, correct privately.

Remember the "50–50 deal" we struck at the beginning of this book, where I promised to express ideas in a highly opinionated fashion and you (hopefully) committed to considering these ideas with an open mind? Well, here's an opportunity for us both to live up to our commitments. Are you ready?

I invite you to consider this: When trying to nurture a respectful workplace culture, keep in mind that what's done in public is corrected in public. And yes, in case you were wondering, this means that in the above scenario, you would respond publicly and on the spot.

I realize that in suggesting this, I'm bumping up against a tradition that is ancient and honored. As early as 35 BC, the Latin writer Publilius Syrus asserted, "Admonish your friends privately, but praise them openly." In the eighteenth century, Russia's Catherine the Great stated, "I like to praise and reward loudly, to blame quietly." And Vince Lombardi, the famed football coach, shared that his recipe for team success relied on the "praise in public and criticize in private" paradigm.

There are good reasons why this rule has gained such traction. It helps maintain people's sense of dignity. It helps avoid resistance and anger among team members who witness their colleague being criticized in public. And let's face it, people respond better to criticism when there is no observer to complicate how they react to the events: The presence of an observer changes the dynamics of any situation.

But here's the catch: When it comes to maintaining a civil, respectful workplace, the correct in private notion is not only flawed, it is potentially harmful. When public behavior that is uncivil or offensive takes place with no response from management, the message is clear: Go ahead, break the window! It's perfectly all right!

If it is you standing there, in that moment you are the embodiment and messenger representing the organization's values, mission and commitment to its employees. You may be telling yourself that you are too frozen and unsure to take action, but the truth is that you are taking action. The action you are taking is this: You are condoning the behavior by remaining silent.

When management does not correct behavior publicly, employees will rightfully conclude that the uncivil (or harassing, or bullying) behavior is condoned. Can you hear the shattering sound of your company's windows as they break?

If you are experiencing a strong reaction to my assertion that your role as a leader requires you to (sometimes) respond in public, and if you are in fact thinking that I may have lost touch with reality and are considering closing this book and never ever reopening it, you are not alone. Having worked with thousands of managers in training on respectful workplace matters, I can share with you that this strategy is the single most controversial of anything I teach. It is exceedingly difficult to let go of your preconceived notions and inner barriers and accept that, whether you like it or not, the business of minding windows includes acting publicly—appropriately, respectfully and effectively.

Other Advantages to Correcting in Public

When handled correctly, a public response to incivility stops the undesirable behavior, right then and there. It is unlikely that persons who have been confronted about their conduct in a specific situation will repeat the same behavior later on. On the other hand, if you don't correct publicly, chances are that the behavior will be repeated by the same person or that it will influence the behavior of others and the culture.

Furthermore, responding in public offers you an invaluable opportunity to set the standard, for all to grasp and follow. Not only are you setting the standard, you are also reinforcing key organizational values. Conversely, standing there and doing nothing conveys the message that values such as respect, community and integrity (which often form part of an organization's declared values) mean nothing at all on the ground.

When you take a stand, people may not like it in the moment, but it certainly engenders respect toward you as a leader. It establishes your personal leadership brand. And with a brand of this nature, people are more likely to come to you in future with issues that need attention. They will trust your integrity and courage to do the right thing.

BARRIERS TO RESPONDING IN PUBLIC

It's easy enough to say that what's done in public is corrected publicly, but in real life there are several formidable barriers with which you will need to contend. At the heart of these barriers lie your own attitudes and fears, which interfere with getting things done right.

A key culprit is the innate human need to be liked. Whether you admit it to yourself or not, as a human being you are driven by a strong need for love, approval and appreciation. In fact, if you take time to reflect on your actions in the past three or four hours with brutal honesty, you will readily find at least ten things that you did or said to attract love, approval or appreciation. It could have been as small as splashing on some aftershave or applying your makeup, or perhaps telling someone that he or she looked great when they didn't really look that great, or writing an email that made you look witty or compassionate. One way or another, you were seeking these responses.

Responding in public to correct someone's behavior automatically places you at risk of being less liked, or not liked at all. This alone might freeze you and render you unable to take action in the moment when it is most needed.

In a unionized environment, there is an additional layer. Here, managers are particularly concerned that correcting behavior in public will lead to a grievance or harassment complaint against them. This is one of the most common concerns that managers raise in my training sessions when we discuss the need to fix windows by correcting publicly. My response is always the same: If you do it right, following the guidelines I suggest, you will not trigger union upset. You will be able to demonstrate that you performed your duty thoughtfully and carefully, while maintaining everyone's dignity.

As well, there is the valid hesitation about how and what exactly one should do when responding in public. The fear of not getting it right and creating further upset can be crippling. Managers (and even veteran HR professionals) are not sure exactly how to respond. And without the skill set, they tend to avoid doing anything altogether.

Finally, most situations involving offensive or crossing-the-line behavior happen very fast. It may be a comment, a sneer, a joke, a gesture. The speed at which things happen, often in the midst of a busy environment, makes it difficult to respond immediately. By the time your mind registers the occurrence and your canary sends its alert, and by the time you run through some form of the banner litmus test in your mind and then figure out what exactly you ought to do or say, the moment is often gone.

MISTAKES TO AVOID

There are three common mistakes to avoid when responding in public to any sort of incivility (or, for that matter, harassment).

First, I-statements. The term "I-statement" refers to a specific type of assertive communication in which the speaker provides another person with a candid glimpse of how that person's behavior made the speaker feel. For example, "I felt excluded when you continued speaking your native language with Mirjana even though I was sitting beside you."

I-statements can serve as a very powerful communication tool (we will discuss them in depth later on, in chapter 15, when we look at incivility that is directed toward you personally.) However, they are neither appropriate nor useful when your goal as someone who represents institutional authority is to correct behavior, especially in public. The purpose of correcting offensive behavior is to create common standards and to enforce organizational values. Whether or not you personally were offended is, frankly, irrelevant. Therefore, don't say, "I was offended by that joke." Instead say, "Jokes that focus on people's physical attributes are not appropriate in our environment."

Second, avoid the common pitfall of attempting to use humor when correcting in public. Humor is a wonderful tool, but when it comes to correcting behavior, using humor runs the risk that your message will not get across or will not be taken seriously and, therefore, the desired change will not happen. Furthermore, you are running the risk that rather than being funny, you yourself will be offensive. It is exceedingly difficult to get the exact right note with humor. You can use a light touch, but trying to stop behavior by using pure humor is counterproductive and in fact might boomerang.

Finally, never dispute the accuracy or content of whatever has been said. If someone makes a comment that characterizes a particular ethnic group as having certain characteristics, for example, never say,

"Well, actually, that is factually incorrect. The truth is that people of this group..." By doing so, you are inadvertently expanding and deepening the offensive discussion that stereotypes groups of people and making it a topic of discussion. Besides, you're opening the door to a debate, and chances are that you'll find yourself losing.

OBJECTIVES AND CONSIDERATIONS WHEN YOU GO PUBLIC

Responding in public is easier to do if you have clear objectives in mind. Every situation is unique and different, yet by and large the objectives you should have in mind when you intervene in public should always include the following:

1. **Stop the behavior.** Whatever you do, you must convey the message that the behavior has got to stop. Therefore, be very clear about your request for it to stop, and ensure your tone and body language communicate the same message. If, for example, your verbal communication is "Eye-rolling is not okay. Let's not go there!" then make sure that you lift your head and look the person in the eye so that your body language also conveys "stop."

2. **Maintain everyone's dignity.** It's very easy to intervene in a harsh way that ends up being hurtful or degrading to the other person, adding insult to injury. Whatever you do has to maintain the other person's (or persons') dignity. Therefore, make sure to use language and a tone that convey respect and collegiality.

   One of the best strategies for maintaining everyone's dignity is to do what I call the Intervene-Switch move. Here's how it works (when appropriate): Once you have said what you have to say to correct the behavior, you immediately change the topic to a very light, controversy-free topic that everyone can relate to, such as the weather, an upcoming big concert or sports event, or a news item that everyone is excited about, then finish up with a question that invites everyone to comment.

An Intervene-Switch might sound like this:

"On our team, respect for each other's opinions is part of who we are. Telling someone you don't have time to listen to their blabber doesn't fit with that, so let's not go there. Now, what's the latest news on the big storm, is it expected to land tonight or tomorrow?"

Using this strategy enables everyone to breathe a sigh of relief, knowing that you have taken care of whatever needed to be addressed (your broken window) and now everyone can move safely on.

3. **Preserve the relationship.** Workplace relationships can easily sour. A wrong word or gesture can trigger long-lasting resentment that will make it difficult to maintain a productive relationship with this employee later on. So whatever you do when you respond in public, remember that your objective is to preserve (and possibly even strengthen) the relationship, not ruin it. Avoid accusatory language or diagnostic terms and stick to video-camera terms as discussed earlier, in chapter 10. If you are concerned about the impact of your intervention, follow up afterward to ensure that no hard feelings remain.

An awareness of these objectives will help you maintain the right tone and approach and you will, as a consequence, achieve more effective results.

CORRECTING PUBLICLY is a delicate and complex affair. Later on, in chapter 14, we will review a wide range of verbal responses to choose from in any given situation. For the purposes of examining how to achieve best results when responding in public, let's touch here on three types of choices you'll always need to make:

- **Now or later?** There's always the question of whether you should respond immediately or later. When it comes to incivility that is performed in public, whenever possible, it is best to respond in the moment. Sometimes a combination of now and later is required.

- **Light touch or heavy-handed?** Some situations require a light-touch response. Others require a heavy-handed one. When responding in public, the lighter and more informal the approach, the better. It is particularly useful to use the word "we" rather than "you," as it avoids blame and puts everyone in the same boat. So, for example, you might say, "Guys, we don't swear around here; let's cut it out," instead of, "Tom, this type of talk is unacceptable, and in fact constitutes harassment under our harassment policy."

- **Short or long?** With your eyes fixed on the objective of maintaining everyone's dignity, the shorter the response, the better. This makes it clear that your purpose is to make a point and move on. If you take a longer approach, there is a good chance that you will start meandering, go in circles and lose it altogether.

GOING PUBLIC, STEP-BY-STEP

Let's return to the case at the beginning of this chapter. To refresh your memory, you joined several people by the coffee machine, and a staff member from another department questioned the work of someone who was not present, in a snippy tone. There were in the group two people who reported to you, one from another department, one unfamiliar employee and a total stranger.

This scenario demonstrates clearly why it is important to respond in public, in the moment. What if the person carrying the briefcase is a highly talented job candidate, about to step into a pivotal job interview? If you do not respond to the nasty comment, this interaction will shape this person's impression of what your organization stands for in a much more indelible way than any fancy mission statement you may have hanging on every wall. For all we know, based on this interaction alone and your condoning of it, this person may choose to take the job that your competitor is offering rather than join the ranks of your organization.

Furthermore, the two people who report to you will observe you standing there and doing nothing. This will deeply affect their view of your leadership and your commitment to a respectful workplace. If they already have a poor perception of you, this will certainly strengthen that perception. If they have a more neutral or even positive perspective on your leadership, they will be deeply disappointed, but may never share their disappointment directly with you. And you can be sure that they will not be likely to bring to your attention any similar situations in future, because they will perceive you as incompetent in these types of circumstances.

So how should you respond in this scenario?

The best option will be to keep the intervention very short and use the Intervene-Switch strategy. Keep a light touch, while referring to the organization's values. The S-B-D feedback structure described earlier in chapter 10 might serve you well here.

Putting all these factors together, you might move physically closer to the others having this conversation, look the speaker in the eye briefly, then redirect your gaze and say very clearly, such that everyone can hear: "Let's not go there!" Pause for a second and change the topic, now looking at no one in particular.

Or you could use a longer and more detailed approach. Looking at no one in particular, you might say:

"Excuse me, I couldn't help but overhear the conversation. I'd like to point out that around here, when we have issues, we deal directly with the people involved. Let's not talk about anyone who's not here right now. Now, is this coffee fresh or should we brew a fresh batch?"

Responding to incivility or other respect-related situations in public is always challenging. I have worked with very senior leaders who often have the same difficulty in doing so as a newly minted frontline supervisor. In these situations, the powerful inner voices that prevent you from being sure of yourself and taking immediate action are loud, almost deafening. Still, it is something you need to do in your role as a leader. And doing it right will make all the difference in the world.

IMPLEMENTATION CLINIC

Go Public: Fix Windows on the Spot

Correcting behavior in public can cause you anxiety and fear. It may shake your need to be liked and appreciated, and will certainly seem contradictory to the basic management golden rule of "Praise in public, correct in private."

To intervene successfully in uncivil behavior that takes place in public, keep the following objectives in mind:

1. Stop the behavior.

2. Maintain everyone's dignity.

3. Preserve the relationship(s).

Whenever possible, choose a light and informal tone, use "we" language and change the topic immediately after delivering the crux of your message.

To prepare yourself to respond quickly in the moment the next time around, reflect on the following questions:

1. Find an example of a situation where you should have responded in public and didn't. As you reflect on the situation, consider:
    a. Did your inner canary get activated?
    b. What thoughts, concerns or worries stopped you from taking action in the moment?
    c. Over time, how did not taking action affect you?

    d. Were you aware of any impact that the situation had on those involved or otherwise? If so, what was the impact?
    e. In hindsight, what would you have done differently?
2. What will it take for you to be able to respond in public and on the spot when it is appropriate to do so? What changes do you need to make? What preparation will it take, mentally or in terms of practical skill building?

*　*　*

12

MAKING EVERYONE CARE
CREATE A CIVIL TEAM CULTURE

....

TAKING ACTION TO BOOST TEAM CIVILITY

Some team contexts provide richer, more fertile ground for workplace incivility than others. On one end of the spectrum you will find teams where rude, insensitive or discourteous behavior is the norm. At the opposite end are team environments that discourage and repel incivility. As described in chapter 1, team cultures run the full gamut, from Healthy Body, through Persistent Allergy and Chronic Infection, right up to Acute Disease.

Your role as a leader is to build, support and maintain a professional environment. This means that team members act with high levels of accountability, self-regulate their emotions, maintain an even-keeled demeanor even under pressure, demonstrate teamwork and behave in a courteous manner to both colleagues and customers. The level of professionalism that people demonstrate has nothing to do with education or skill levels; it's all about attitude and culture. High levels of professionalism create a strong fabric that serves as a barrier to the rise of incivility.

If you are lucky (or smart) enough to lead a team where incivility is minor, the task you face is relatively simple. However, if the team you lead is highly uncivil, the task of boosting civility and professionalism can be daunting. Some individuals on your team might seem to loom large, and their conduct and power within the group will make you fearful of taking them on. In fact, you may feel discouraged and not know where to start and what to do. (In the next chapter we will examine what exactly you can and should do to address chronically uncivil individual behavior.)

So let's look at what you can do on the prevention and maintenance front, and then check out best strategies for dealing with long-standing team incivility issues.

PREVENTION AND MAINTENANCE TOUCHSTONES

There is truth to the old adage, a rotten apple can easily spoil the barrel. You should never assume that if the culture of the team you lead is civil, then it is immune to an incivility invasion.

Prevention is key to success. It mitigates future problems and empowers team members to take care of things themselves (while you will be free to tend to other matters). Below are things you can do on the prevention front.

Surface Issues Before They Become Problems

Civility problems on a team, like mines in a minefield, can be detected and cleared well before they have a chance to explode and hurt someone.

I once worked with a group of managers who were recovering from a couple of employee-to-employee harassment situations that took them by surprise. They were shocked that within their healthy organizational culture such things could occur. Upon reflection, they realized that many of the problematic situations could have been surfaced earlier had they paid a little more attention and been more proactive. They also recognized that these situations sprouted much earlier with behaviors that could be classified as incivility rather than harassment.

Together, we developed a simple scanning tool to help them detect potential respect-related issues well before they wreak havoc. They then incorporated this new tool into the monthly check-in meetings that managers and supervisors were already conducting with each employee. (Interventions tend to work well when they are piggybacked onto processes that are part of the existing organizational rhythm.)

You, too, might find the questions we developed useful; experiment with asking them and see what you discover. If the answers yield any hint of trouble, follow up with additional probing questions. Of course, if the answers indicate that the environment is highly respectful, it will also be beneficial to inquire into what works well; knowing what makes the culture respectful will help you reinforce positive behavior and will serve to inoculate the culture against potential problems.

Table 9: Scanning Tool for Team Civility

> Here are the questions you can explore to scan for team civility:
>
> "It's my role, and the organization's responsibility, to ensure that we maintain a respectful work environment where everyone can work without fear or concern. In that vein, I'd like to check in with you on the following:
>
> - On a scale of 1 to 10, how would you rate the overall respect in the work environment (team, division, organization)?
> - On a scale of 1 to 10, how respected do you feel these days?
> - What would make you give a higher rating on the scale?
> - Over the last while, has anyone said or done anything that made you feel uncomfortable or disrespected? If they ever do, please let me, or HR, or anyone else in management know, so that we can fix things without delay."

Clarify Roles

A company engaged our services to address interpersonal conflicts on a particular team. Through our assessment process we discovered that much of the conflict and its associated incivility stemmed from lack of clarity about individual roles on the team. People had a blurred sense of the specific responsibilities associated with their respective roles, especially during night shift when the manager was not around. As a result, they were constantly overstepping each other's boundaries and causing personal irritation, which manifested in a range of uncivil behavior and retaliatory aggression (which, by the way, were done in plain view of the nighttime clients). The first intervention was, therefore, to redefine and clarify each role and the interfaces between the roles. This in itself alleviated a significant part of the incivility.

Lack of role is a common and usually overlooked trigger of workplace incivility. When your people are not clear where the interface between their respective roles begins and ends, resentments and negative perceptions naturally emerge. All too often we have been called in to assist with conflict resolution or incivility, only to discover that the issues are rooted in confusion about roles.

Ensure that job responsibilities are clearly defined. A red flag should come up for you whenever employees are behaving in an uncivil fashion while concurrently complaining about territory-related matters, or griping about how the actual work is being performed. In these instances, before addressing the incivility itself, begin by asking some probing questions, such as:

"I hear your concern about Nancy not doing her fair share. Help me understand. As you see it, when this type of work process happens, what exactly are you responsible for—what are your tasks? What do you think

Nancy's part is? Are there overlaps? Are you picking up things that you think she should be doing in her role?"

Incivility can be the result of upset over territory; your role as the manager is to create and define clear responsibilities and job descriptions, then ensure that everyone understands and follows their roles.

Create Team Norms

The terms "team norms," "team charter" and "team operating agreement" refer to a set of principles, ideas and behaviors that everyone on the team consensually agrees to follow. Through a process of discussion and dialogue, team members generate the content of the team charter themselves. It's surprising how the process of creating and sustaining a (good) norms document can change even long-standing problematic team dynamics.

The first objective that team norms achieve is defining the behaviors that people commit to demonstrating. Clarity is crucial—make sure your norms go beyond broad declarations, such as "We treat each other with respect" or "We communicate with one another openly and honestly." Ask anyone and they'll tell you that they want to work and contribute to a respectful environment, but everyone's interpretation of what this actually means is so very different. Broad declarations are wonderful in that they set a tone and define aspirations, but the charter also needs to describe the specific ways in which these behaviors will manifest.

To identify specific behaviors that will give life to the larger declaratory ideas, create dialogue around the following type of questions: What will we see and hear that will let us know that we respect each other? What would a video camera capture that would indicate that we are respectful?"

So, for example, rather than saying only "We treat each other with respect," you might agree on:

We demonstrate our respect for each other through the following actions:

- *We do not gossip or spread rumors.*
- *We sincerely apologize when we have offended or upset another.*
- *We do not use sarcasm.*
- *We acknowledge peers, say hello, and thank each other.*
- *Our body language is respectful and attentive.*

There is no real harm in adding some items that are a bit more generic (such as "We accept others as they are"), so long as there are sufficient specific and detailed behaviors similar to those listed above and so long as you do not arrive at a set of aspirational yet intangible statements that end up gathering dust on some remote bulletin board.

The second objective for the charter is to help team members hold each other (and themselves) accountable to the behaviors to which they aspire, and to help you, the leader, to do so too. So make sure you decide together on the ways in which people will hold each other to their commitments, and clarify what your role as the leader will be in this regard.

Team norms will work only if you keep the agreement alive as an active document that people actually live by. I have seen too many teams that have spent time, effort and precious dollars on creating beautifully crafted norms but the values and behaviors that are written up in the document are violated on a daily basis. In the hustle and bustle of work life, it is difficult to find the time and space to revisit the norms, revise them as necessary and hold each other accountable for the agreed-upon commitments. However, if you do not put in place systems to keep it alive, the document will become just one more of those well-intended, dead-end initiatives.

There are a number of things you can do to increase accountability and keep the norms active:

- Post the norms in people's workstations (and certainly on yours) as a constant reminder.
- Post a handsome-looking copy of the norms in locations that are clearly visible to your customers. It makes team members more self-aware, and it enables outsiders to hold your people to the desirable behavior standards.
- Place the norms on the agenda for quarterly or semiannual team events for check-in, review, reflection and revisions.
- Begin team meetings with a quick review of the norms and/or end with a five-minute discussion period to review the extent to which the meeting upheld the charter's commitments. Place the check-ins as agenda items and ensure that those several minutes actually take place.
- Include the norms in the onboarding process for new hires. Pair the new team member with a mentor, a peer on the team, who will go over the document with them and keep it top of mind during the initial period on the job and beyond.
- Include discussion of the norms in your one-on-one meetings with people, and especially during performance reviews.
- Ask people informally for their view on how well the team is doing in upholding the norms.
- Distribute brief (anonymous) surveys that allow people to express their view and concerns about how well the team is living up to its values.

Well-constructed team norms inspire a sense of empowerment to address uncivil behavior that is incongruent with the norms. By the way, having a set of norms in place by no means gets you, the leader, off the hook. You will still need to tend to uncivil behavior as it arises, using all the strategies in this book as well as any other strategies that you devise yourself.

Educate

Here's where education is important: Most people are not aware when they come across as rude, insensitive or discourteous. Bringing this behavior to their attention in a supportive way can propel positive change.

Education begins with you, the leader. You are the one who is intimately aware of the organization's values and aspirations. You are the one who is committed to creating a civil work environment. You are the one who knows what the uncivil behaviors are and can outline what behaviors should replace them. (And yes, you are the one leading by walking the talk.)

Start by assuming that people do not have the knowledge or awareness to grasp fully what civility can and should look like. Therefore, educate by starting from the very foundational concepts and build up from there. Do so through team discussion, personal conversations, written communication or other team activities—make increasing the team's awareness and practice of civility an ongoing, supportive process of teaching and inspiring.

Teach Skills for Handling Sticky Situations

Sticky situations are interpersonal interactions that if not handled well can lead to full-blown conflict or otherwise damage a relationship. For example, Adam might feel resentful toward Nelia, whom he perceives to have befriended their manager in order to be selected for a plum assignment. His feelings about this could sour their working relationship for years to come and yet Adam keeps procrastinating about speaking directly with Nelia about the events and his reactions. At the same time, acting on his upset feelings, he starts making sarcastic comments about her work. This uncivil behavior triggers further mutual incivility (the spiral effect that we discussed in chapter 2) and potentially serious damage to the relationship.

Dealing with sticky situations directly and constructively can be exceedingly challenging for anyone on your staff (and for you too). People have an aversion to conflict, so they avoid dealing with it openly. Instead, they handle things by venting to another colleague, gossiping or retaliating. In short, as part of their handling of the sticky situation, they unintentionally engage in workplace incivility.

If you are comfortable intervening in these kinds of situations yourself, you can teach or coach your people on how they can handle sticky situations on their own, constructively and assertively. If you feel unable to do so, then expert training is an excellent solution. Attend the training alongside the team to improve your proficiency in dealing with sensitive interpersonal matters and to help you support and coach the team by leveraging what they learned.

Bring in Civility Training for the Team

A good training experience will provide everyone with a skill-building opportunity. Ideally, you should attend leader-specific civility training while your staff attends their own sessions. At Bar-David Consulting, we always recommend doing so because leaders require learning of a different skill set than staff members.

Training for staff is an excellent idea that's relatively simple to implement. When considering whom you should hire, do your due diligence to ensure that the company you engage is reputable and offers specific expertise in the area of workplace incivility. Look for highly interactive training (there's way too much talking-to that happens in many respect-in-the-workplace workshops) and inquire about the specific methods the trainer will use to get your staff inspired and motivated.

Make Civility a Top-of-Mind Topic

Encourage an environment in which civility is discussed on a regular basis. For example, include references to it in communications that you send out, especially those that are sent out in written form. If you have a team or company newsletter, publish ideas, stories and articles about civility. Praise the team for being civil and discuss situations where civility made a difference to the work or to the environment. Congratulate specific people personally or in writing for civil behaviors and the positive impact that they have had.

Make Civility Fun

Creating fun and buzz around taming incivility will go a long way in warming people up to the topic and keeping it top of mind. If your team is blessed with people who are good at inventing games and creating fun activities, enlist them to assist in, or be in charge of, making civility fun for everyone. Folks like this will come up with creative ideas that you may not think of yourself. If you do not have such talent on your team, consider initiating such activities on your own (you can find resources for active learning and fun team activities by accessing training or team-learning websites and books and even resources for school teachers).

Coach

With some individuals, you will need to take a coaching approach. This approach is well suited for employees who are intent on changing but require ongoing support to maintain momentum and accountability. If your employer is a larger enterprise, there are likely tools that your organization provides to managers like you to help you have coaching conversations with your staff. If your organization does not offer such resources, you will find a wealth of books and online resources on coaching skills for managers. Using a coaching approach, you can encourage staff to experiment with different behaviors and see what difference they make. This will be a rewarding process for both the person receiving the coaching and for you.

Other times you might use a coaching approach to help individuals who come to you with a concern about a colleague's incivility. Rather than immediately intervening, you can coach this person (and possibly even role play) on how he or she might solve the problem himself or herself.

Mediate

Sometimes the level of incivility between two or more individuals has reached a point where mediation will be necessary. (Hopefully, after having read this far into the book, you now know that you should intervene long before things get even remotely close to this.) The upset and hurt between these individuals might have led to communication breakdowns, creation of supporters' camps and disruptions to the work.

If you feel comfortable mediating between the parties involved, go ahead and do so. If you don't feel comfortable, bring in an external expert. The most important factor to include in the intervention, whether it is implemented by you or by external consultants, is this:

The people involved need to understand in no uncertain terms that the organization expects them to behave in a professional fashion regardless of their upset or resentments. You will need to communicate very clearly that incivility or disruptions to the work will not be tolerated and what the consequences will be should the behavior persist after the intervention. Employees are certainly entitled to have negative feelings, but while in your employ they cannot act on these feelings in any visibly uncivil ways. Conduct needs to reflect decorum, politeness and mutual respect at all times.

DEALING WITH CHRONIC TEAM INCIVILITY

Life is wonderful when you take on leadership of a team that is consistently civil and productive. In real life, things don't always unfold in that way. In real life, you may have inherited a team that is uncivil. You may have attempted various solutions and even seen some success, but not sufficient to fundamentally change the unproductive dynamics.

Or possibly you are the leader of a team that over time developed bad habits without you paying much attention. One not-so-fine day you look around and realize that things are not at all as they should be. Or, alternatively, perhaps you did notice the deterioration over time but did nothing (and likely got yourself off the hook by using a range of excuses that you allowed yourself to believe).

Changing the culture of a chronically uncivil work group requires special effort. In these teams, people have become desensitized to persistent and dysfunctional interactional patterns. They are blind to the damage that the culture is inflicting on themselves and others, including those whom they serve. These behaviors are held in place because under the surface there is an undercurrent of incivility-supporting beliefs (some of which we discussed in chapter 5) and these beliefs are exceedingly difficult to both name and tackle. In trying to change these teams you will be going against ingrained habits, familiar ways of interacting and being, and a calcified status quo. It takes years for such an environment to establish itself, and your attempts to change things will be met by the natural forces of inertia and resistance. Any homeostasis, even when it is neither pleasant nor productive, is difficult to change. You are up against formidable dynamics, so real change will require an abundance of focus, perseverance, patience and even courage.

The first step is to identify the specific protracted behaviors that manifest on your team (refer to the list of uncivil behaviors covered in chapter 1). Try to diagnose the level of incivility using the disease framework I outlined in that chapter: Is your team in a state of Chronic Infection or has it reached the level of Acute Disease? Or perhaps it is suffering from Persistent Allergy that will become more acute if not tended to?

To prepare for the journey of shifting the culture, begin by focusing on the following:

- **Vision and clarity.** To get your team out of its rut, you will need to be able to inspire yourself and then inspire others to come along on the journey with you.

    Begin by developing in your own mind a palpable vision for a future civil team. Get a crystal-clear image of what you will see and hear that will indicate that your team is civil. In your imagination, run through all the activities, tasks, physical spaces and social interactions that your group experiences in the course of a given day and ask yourself what will be different about each of these once civility sets in.

    Cultivate your inner resolve by clarifying for yourself why all this matters in the first place. Is it the need to increase the team's performance and its customer service capabilities? Are you driven by wanting to do the right thing? Are you concerned that if things don't change, there's potential for harassment and bullying to emerge? Identify your core reasons and keep them top of mind throughout the process.

With such clarity and resolve, you will now be able to mobilize others.

- **Underlying beliefs.** Below the surface of any chronically uncivil team culture lie shared incivility-enabling beliefs that keep that uncivil culture going. These beliefs perpetuate and feed the culture. If you don't tackle them, you will not achieve lasting culture change.

  Make sure to identify the specific beliefs that your team shares. For starters, review which of the beliefs outlined in chapter 5 apply and what other unique ones characterize your team. Often the beliefs are right there in plain view if you only take the time to listen to the way people express themselves. For example, someone might say in passing, "I love how we can be so frank with each other, without having to worry about choosing every word." When people hold this shared belief, you will see unduly harsh treatment of others under the guise of being frank. With some careful listening and a bit of probing, you will find the answers.

- **Barriers**. Identify the barriers that you might encounter in your effort to change the culture and plan how you will address each of these barriers. (Refer to the list in table 10 for an overview of barrier categories.)

Table 10: Barriers to Changing a Chronically Uncivil Team Culture

> Barriers to changing a chronically uncivil team culture fall under the following categories:
>
> - **People-related barriers.** These can show up, for example, in the form of resistance from the team or from specific members who have become accustomed to behaving in certain ways. Or in some cases, the person who is the most noticeable "offender" has significant seniority and would be hard to take on.
> - **Time-related barriers.** You'll encounter these when, for example, you can't quite find the time necessary to dedicate to initiating the change or seeing it through. Another time-related challenge emerges when you are physically not there to observe things with your own eyes. This is often the case in healthcare or other environments where the manager is not on-site during after-hours shifts.
> - **Context-related hindrances.** These present themselves when, for example, your team or some of its members work virtually and you cannot observe the incivility as it occurs nor respond effectively. Another context-related issue is when a key uncivil player happens to be president of the local union and any attempt to take on this person might unnecessarily escalate into a serious labor relations matter.

Taking Action on the Ground

Having done some of the preparation, it is now time to address the chronic issues that plague your team. The stakes are high and the status quo is established, so you will need to invest extra thought and effort into the strategies discussed in the book thus far—minding the windows, walking the talk, listening to your canary, applying the line test, providing corrective feedback, responding to situations in public and following the team-specific strategies provided right here in this chapter. To increase your chances of success at changing the team's chronically uncivil culture, pay special attention to the following:

- **Explain the change.** Explain what led you to change your approach to incivility (and take responsibility for not having done so previously). As much as possible, connect this with the overarching organizational values and aspired culture. For example, "In our workplace, respect for each other's expertise is a key principle."

- **Get them involved.** Changing the culture will only be possible if people buy the idea that change is necessary and they can see the logic in how the change will be achieved. Developing a sense of ownership is crucial to changing the problematic culture. If you do not tend to this, strong resistance and sabotage are bound to emerge, much more so than in circumstances where the incivility is not chronic. Therefore, involve as many team members as possible, in meaningful ways, in your efforts.

- **Intervene continuously.** Whether you like it or not, turning the direction of the tide will require you to find the time and gumption to address incivility regularly, formally and informally, frequently, publicly and in private. "Continuously" is the operating principle on this front. Keep at it—you can make it happen!

- **Deal with chronic offenders.** The culture of a chronically uncivil team is often driven by the behavior of one or two habitually uncivil individuals. Therefore, dealing with those individuals will be key to your success in changing the team culture.

- **Hold frank performance appraisals.** Frank performance reviews are an imperative to the fundamental change you need to make.

Address civility in everyone's performance appraisals—provide positive feedback to those who are upholding civility and demand change of those whose behavior requires improvement.

IN THIS CHAPTER we discussed a range of strategies you can use to create a strong fabric of civility within your team, even when the problems are chronic. But what about tackling the behavior of a specific team member whose behavior is chronically uncivil? Well, let's take a look at this very issue in the next chapter.

IMPLEMENTATION CLINIC

Intervening on the Team Level

You will need to take action continuously at the team level to boost civility. Some of your efforts will focus on prevention. Other times, you'll need to implement changes to fix ongoing or chronic incivility problems that you inherited or that may have developed while you were leading the group.

As you prepare to make the necessary changes to strengthen the team's culture, you may want to work on:

1. **Clarity:** What is your palpable vision for a civil team? What compelling images will you convey to your people that will make them want to buy into your vision? Why do you want to make these changes? What is truly driving you?

2. **Self-scan:** Which of your own behaviors do you need to change before you have the moral authority to ask others to change?

3. **Shared beliefs:** What counterproductive beliefs permeate the team culture and enable or perpetuate incivility?

4. **Barriers:** What type of challenges (people-related, time-related, context-related) are you likely to encounter as you work on civility issues with your team?

You will need to tend to any or all of the following:

- Surfacing issues early and proactively
- Clarifying roles
- Creating team norms

- Educating, coaching and mediating
- Teaching skills for handling sticky situations
- Bringing in training
- Making civility a top-of-mind topic (and fun too)
- Intervening continuously
- Dealing with chronic offenders
- Holding frank performance appraisals

* * *

13

DOWN IN THE TRENCHES
DEALING WITH CHRONICALLY UNCIVIL INDIVIDUALS

....

IT'S TIME TO STEP UP AND DEAL WITH IT

Dealing with individuals who have a long track record of uncivil behaviors will be both trying and challenging. Over the years, numerous managers have shared with me their great frustration and helplessness in dealing with such employees. This chapter will help you avoid such frustration and manage these situations effectively.

What differentiates a chronically uncivil employee? Here are the top ten things to look for:

1. The uncivil behavior is repetitive and predictable.

2. The incivility is part of an ingrained style of relating to others, to the extent that others (and sometimes even the person in question) perceive it as a personality trait.

3. The person has periods (hours, days, weeks) of being excessively uncivil. People might say, "You don't want to be on shift with George when he's in one of his foul moods."

4. The behaviors are intense and more serious than the more common forms of workplace incivility. For example, door slamming, using

objects to display displeasure (clicking a pen loudly in a meeting to express disapproval) or unmistakably dismissive body gestures that are meant to be seen as such.

5. There seems to be intent behind the behavior—often without the person bothering to hide it.

6. When provided with feedback on his or her uncivil behavior, the person has a strong negative reaction, and typically does not change as a result of the feedback.

7. When provided with feedback, the response is along the lines of "Well, that's just who I am, it's my personality" or "That's your problem, not mine."

8. The uncivil behavior demonstrates disregard for authority, involving behaviors that others would consider to be too risky. Here you will find anything from using foul language when relating to a manager to publicly belittling a manager's ideas, initiatives, judgment or personality. (In certain instances, the repetitive nature of these behaviors over time and the intimidation that they create in the manager amount to workplace bullying.)

9. The person takes retaliatory action when someone provides them with feedback they do not like, as well as taking it against anyone who complains about their behavior to management.

10. The person's uncivil behavior is protected, sanctioned and sometimes cheered by a cluster of "groupies" whose allegiance was developed over many years of working together; these people might complain about the person's behavior to a manager but are afraid to take him or her on and instead act as an applauding audience.

Managing people who practice these behaviors is, to say the least, challenging. It can feel like they have more power than you do, even though you possess more institutional authority. There's always the potential for a blowback of even more negative behavior in reaction to being confronted on poor conduct. It takes time to manage them and to manage the situation. They are expert at behaviors that are exceedingly problematic yet hard to nail down. In short, it's a bit of a Sisyphean task.

Let's face it, dealing with chronically uncivil persons, like dealing with any other performance issue, is right up there on any manager's list of most despised tasks. Many managers avoid dealing with chronic cases. They procrastinate over days, months and years. You, too, may have fallen into this trap and found seemingly good reasons for staying in it. You might be very busy. Or you may have a personal relationship with this person. Perhaps you know that the individual is struggling with difficult personal circumstances and you do not want to make things more difficult for him or her. In other cases, the person in question might possess unique expertise and you are concerned that if you address the incivility, he or she might leave the organization and take the expertise with them. Or perhaps you're paralyzed by the fear that if you raise the issues, the person will overpower you or you might otherwise botch the conversation. Meanwhile, things on the ground get worse. The uncivil behaviors get entrenched, other team members begin to question your leadership and business suffers.

Still, you need to change things. Many times along this journey you will question why you are undertaking it in the first place and wish you never ever started with this process. At these times, you may wish to reread the first part of this book to remind yourself why civility really matters. Or perhaps you can find comfort in recalling when a problem individual changed his or her behavior for the better and in remembering how rewarding that was. Or maybe you can find strength in thinking about a situation where you did let someone go and their dismissal had an enormous positive impact on the team, the environment and the work.

BEFORE ALL ELSE: OWN MANAGEMENT'S CONTRIBUTION TO THE PROBLEM

A senior leader in a large, unionized healthcare center emailed me to ask this:

"When a manager begins to take decisive action to address long-standing problem behavior, how should leaders handle the strong reactions expressed by employees with a long record of incivility? A few managers who report to me decided after the training we had with you to finally take action with some long-standing problem employees who have for years been intimidating others and creating a poisoned work environment, and yet, when called to task, these very employees (often with the union's active support) have been expressing upset and outrage, and demanded to know, 'Why do I suddenly have a "problem" after all these years?'"

In this situation, resentment, upset and a spirited demand to know why he or she suddenly has a "problem" are totally understandable from the employee's perspective, and, frankly, are justified. After all, management did nothing all these years and now it is suddenly changing the long-standing rules of the game without warning!

Dear reader, are you ready for one of our little "50–50 deal" moments? If so, get ready, because a strong opinion is coming your way.

The single biggest cause for the uncivil behavior of so-called problem employees is that management has for years allowed the behavior to endure without any meaningful consequences. Had management taken action when the bad behavior first showed up (and that was likely many moons ago), these employees would by now be wonderfully civil contributors, or would be working for an altogether different employer.

Instead of nipping the behavior in the bud, management (and please accept my apology if this includes you) engages in a series of actions that are utterly ineffective or, at best, only partially successful, or they take no action at all. Remembering the typical managerial mistakes I outlined in chapter 4, I would venture to say that some if not all of these are routinely committed in the case of dealing with chronically uncivil employees: bad modeling, slow reaction, fear of taking a stand, favoring the intent of the offending person over the impact it has on others, taking the wrong action and mishandling complaints. Top that up with performance appraisals that bear no mention of the problematic behaviors and you've got full-blown management culpability on your hands.

And if you ask how I can be so sure that management has committed so many missteps, my answer is simple: The proof is in the pudding. The only reason that chronically uncivil employees can keep their job while also behaving miserably is because they are allowed to do so.

As you read this, you might be getting quite frustrated with me, wishing that I could hear you saying, "With all due respect, dear Sharone, you really don't understand a thing! Here in my organization we have an all-powerful union. It is impossible to fire anyone unless they stole money right from our general manager's pocket, in front of at least seventeen witnesses." Or you might be saying, "I've been doing performance management with this person forever and I'm really getting nowhere—this is an unsolvable situation."

And my response to you, dear leader in the trenches, is that as much as my heart goes out to you, I still believe that it can be done, even in difficult circumstances such as yours. Where there is a will, there is a way. Where management is fully committed to its responsibility, it will find a way to do it. Yes, it may cost money and it sure will take effort, but you can do it.

Here's one point where we both may agree: If you are in middle management, it is very possible that you have made sincere and energetic efforts to address chronic situations but encountered resistance from senior management that led to failure to take effective action. Or perhaps you really wanted to take the bull by the horns, but in the context of a larger environment where uncivil behavior is common, it was practically impossible to do so without endangering your own standing and alliances. If any of this is true in your case, my guess is that you are haunted by a lingering sense of dissonance as the organizational context forces you to act in ways that are contradictory to your chirping inner canary. Under these circumstances, you may want to consider whether the organization is the right place for you.

Getting back to management's role in enabling the problem behavior, I hope that you do agree that management shares some—maybe even just a very tiny bit—of the responsibility for the fact that this individual continues to behave in the way that he or she does.

Before you proceed to tackle the problem behavior and the changes he or she is expected to make, I recommend that you begin with owning your contribution. Delivering feedback this way will increase the chances of the employee being able to actually take in what you are saying. You need to get through to the person, and that is practically impossible to do when his or her listening is blocked by the inner thoughts and feelings that consume them. In their eyes, they are being treated unfairly, while you are being hypocritical—all this time you never said anything (of substance) about their behavior and now you're suddenly pretending that it's all only their problem. When people feel this way, they become reactive and resistant, and the process loses much of its chances to succeed.

Communicating in this fashion—admitting that you own part of the problem—has a name: it's called fair and just management and it might sound like this:

- *"You're absolutely right, I/we should have taken action a long time ago and I/we didn't. I wish I/we had!"*

- *"I am increasingly and more fully aware of our organization's responsibility to provide everyone with a safe, healthy work environment* where they can perform at their best, and I intend to be more involved in making sure that we live up to this standard."

- "I know it would have been helpful to you and others to know clearly what's okay and what's not, and for me to follow up on that."

- "I take responsibility for not following through on the expectations in the past as much as I should have."

- "I too will do my part in helping you and everyone else live up to this standard."

- "There are some specific, significant concerns I have and changes I want to discuss with you."

DOING IT, STEP-BY-STEP

In chapter 12 we discussed the need for clarity and resolve. These will be particularly crucial through the process ahead. You will need to be anchored in your conviction that civility matters, and in your resolve to do whatever it takes to make it happen, even if you need to go as far as performance management, discipline and possibly dismissal.

Each case will unfold in very different ways, but you should usually follow several general principles:

1. Stick to it

No matter how challenging the process is emotionally and how time-consuming it might be, do not abandon your efforts midway. Dropping things midway will send the message to the individual (and everyone else) that ultimately you are not serious about change. It will also compromise your personal brand as a leader.

2. **Set aside realistic time**

   Make sure to allot sufficient time in your calendar for the activities that you will need to take on. Meetings with the individual, your own manager, human resources, the union or other players behind the scenes will take time. As well, you will need to find space in your schedule for preparing documentation. If you have had any experiences of this sort, you already know how time-consuming they can be. Preparation in advance for the time aspect of this initiative will reduce your stress in the days to come.

   It is important that your manager understands the time commitment that will be required of you to take care of this matter and that he or she fully endorses this commitment. The hours that you will be spending on meetings and documentation will replace time that you would be spending on other projects, so your manager's expectations of you will need to reflect this understanding. For your own sanity and health, try to avoid spending your personal time in the evening and on weekends on documentation.

3. **Assume they can change**

   With the right approach and support, anyone can change. Especially if they realize that their manager means business and that ultimately their employment could be on the line. If you enter the process trusting in yourself, and believing that the person can change despite their track record, this attitude will permeate your actions and be communicated through your verbal interactions and your body language.

4. **Be compassionate**

   As difficult and uncivil as this person's behavior may have been, you are dealing with a human being who has reasons to behave the way he or she does, and who is now called upon to change long-term habits. This is not an easy time for them. Even as the person may respond in resistant or otherwise difficult ways, try to maintain that sense of compassion to see their side of things.

5. Maintain emotional equanimity

Maintain your calm even when things become difficult and you are challenged (sometimes in very personal ways) by the person whose behavior you are attempting to change, or when you have to deal with grievances and complaints they might bring against you in retaliation. Remind yourself that this is not personal. Become present to your journey as a leader and how you want to be remembered many years from now as your legacy continues to shape itself.

6. Secure your back

Ensure that you are not endangering your own standing or reputation. Consult your manager and (when relevant) your human resources partner before you begin taking action. Get their input, advice and especially their support. Provide your manager with regular updates at appropriate intervals. Things can get tricky, so make sure you take care of yourself.

7. Develop a thorough understanding of policies and processes

You will need to rely on your relevant organizational policies, and specifically on those related to respect in the workplace, code of conduct and performance management policies. In a unionized environment, you would be well advised to understand all the pertinent segments of the collective agreement (you might be surprised by some of the clauses there that may actually be helpful to your cause), as well as the union aspects of performance management, grievances and terminations.

8. **Refer continuously to the larger context**

   Make sure to communicate continuously the broader reasons for your current actions to the person whose behavior you are working on changing. He or she needs to know why the change is happening. It may be that the organization as a whole has decided to take on incivility, or perhaps you decided to change your approach as a result of reading this book and learning about the real-life effects of incivility. Relaying the context and background will provide him or her with the understanding that the changes are both important and inevitable.

9. **Take detailed notes**

   You probably already know about the significance of taking notes whenever you are about to embark on changing an individual's performance. I urge you to pay very careful attention to these notes. If your process leads to a grievance or internal complaint by the uncivil employee, you will be surprised at the level to which you may need to defend your every action. Careful notes, taken immediately after an event or interaction, will make a significant difference. You will be extremely thankful later for having done your due diligence early in the process and on an ongoing basis.

10. **Go into discussions with a plan**

    Changing someone's long-standing behavior requires you to use a range of strategies, ranging from influence to actual performance management. Therefore, thoughtful planning before any conversation will go a long way, especially when it is time to begin talking about consequences for not changing. To assist you in this task, refer to the Implementation Clinic at the end of this chapter for a list of things you'll need to consider before going into any more serious conversations with the person.

11. Use the S-B-D method to provide feedback

In chapter 10, which discusses the S-B-D strategy, I described the merits of taking this approach and how best to use it. Remember that using a structured approach to your feedback will help keep even the most difficult conversation on course, in a constructive and productive fashion. It will also decrease your own stress and potential anxiety as you work through these conversations with the chronically uncivil person, where emotions might fly high and upset and accusations might be coming your way.

12. Use video-speak descriptions

The feedback that you provide to the person should focus on observable behaviors rather than abstract (or quasi-diagnostic) terms. This is important anytime you provide corrective feedback (as described in the earlier discussion regarding the S-B-D feedback) and it is doubly important when you deal with chronic incivility. Avoid using descriptions such as "Your behavior is rude and dismissive." Instead say, "You rolled your eyes when others are speaking" or "You've referred to Sunjay's work as substandard nonsense."

Using video-speak will demonstrate that you are fair. Your language will be void of blame and, therefore, it will not trigger unnecessary defensiveness. Furthermore, the use of behavior-based language makes it easier to see when change takes place. It is hard to pinpoint whether a person has stopped being rude or dismissive, but you sure can see when the employee stops their routine eye-rolling behavior and instead begins referring to colleagues' work in neutral or positive terms.

13. Reinforce desirable behaviors

There's nothing easier than focusing on the things that are not working. In fact, the more we focus on what is not going well, the more it shapes our perceptions—everything we see is colored by negativity. It's easy to forget what is going well and, more importantly, to communicate this to the person whose behavior you are trying to change.

Make sure to share with the employee what you see as civil behaviors that are already taking place. And when change begins occurring, reinforce it immediately and frequently. This will increase the person's motivation and demonstrate your constructive attitude, compassion and understanding.

14. Describe the consequences of not changing

A chronically uncivil employee will not initially understand the seriousness of the situation that he or she is facing. Having been permitted to behave in these ways for a long period of time, this person has likely learned that while management might say all the right things, meaningful action does not follow. Therefore, it is important that you communicate that this time is different, why it is different and what specifically will be the consequences should the employee decide to maintain his or her old ways.

15. Use performance reviews

Use the performance appraisal process as an opportunity to highlight the importance of and urgency to change. And—very importantly—document your concerns (and the problem behaviors) clearly. One complaint that I hear repeatedly from managers is that when they inherit a team that has one or more habitually misbehaved individuals and they (the managers) go through the persons' previous performance reviews, they find impeccable evaluations that make little or no mention of any rude or discourteous conduct. With no case history to build on, they now have to start from scratch. So make sure that you do your due diligence: Discuss the issues during performance evaluations, and then do a great job at documenting the discussion.

16. Access additional resources

In some circumstances, the uncivil behavior is triggered by, or related to, factors that are beyond your expertise or area of influence. For example, excessive stress in a person's personal life can easily trigger uncivil behavior at work, just as a mental health problem can result in a person behaving discourteously on the job.

When these situations present themselves, do not try to solve the problem on your own. You may not be adequately equipped to deal with it and doing so spells nothing but potential trouble. Consult your human resources partner, who will be familiar with additional resources as well as relevant legislation. In some situations, a referral to the employee assistance program might be useful.

Just remember this: You can help the employee reach the required standard through assistance and referral, but the bottom line is that when someone shows up to work, it is a job expectation that he or she behave in a civil fashion.

17. Find a trusted confidant

You will need someone with whom you can discuss matters openly and who can give you honest feedback. If you are lucky enough to have this type of relationship with your manager, then you may not need to look further. However, if you don't share this type of open relationship with your boss, then it might be a good idea to find a confidential source of support elsewhere.

18. Be kind to yourself

If your stress levels are elevated as a result of the time and effort required to change the chronically uncivil person's behavior, make sure to do whatever helps you relieve stress, on the job or at home. At work, make sure that you take small breaks, stretch your body and eat your meals without distraction.

BUT WHAT IF NOTHING CHANGES?

Let's assume for a moment that you have intervened with the person whose behavior is chronically uncivil. And let's assume that you followed the most prudent path and yet nothing has changed, or perhaps the change did not go sufficiently far to ameliorate the problem. Like many others in your position, you might feel discouraged and helpless. You might feel that there is nothing you can do and that you have exhausted your options.

Feeling this way is normal and, in fact, quite characteristic for managers who are dealing with chronically uncivil employees. This is especially so if you are working in a unionized environment where it feels difficult to take action because it might trigger a grievance, or where you believe that it is impossible to fire anyone for problem behavior.

Do not let these feelings drive the agenda. It is your responsibility to ensure that a respectful workplace is maintained. Therefore, if a person does not change in response to your guidance and urging, you will need to escalate the matter and turn the protracted attitude problem into a performance matter. You will need to use the notes that you carefully took throughout the process and commence a performance management process that could even eventually lead to dismissal. True, this is not something you would want to do, but, given all that you now know about the effects of chronic incivility in the workplace, you will have no choice but to take matters as far as you need to.

THUS FAR we have covered all the steps that you can and should take to prevent incivility from happening in the first place, as well as strategies for dealing with chronic situations related to teams and individuals. Next up, what do you do and what are your options when you are called on to deal with a specific situation? Which screwdriver should you choose and when?

IMPLEMENTATION CLINIC

Intervening with Chronically Uncivil Individuals

Dealing with an employee who demonstrates chronic uncivil behaviors will be demanding. It will require work, will encroach on your time, and may place pressure on your emotional reserves.

Owning up to management's role in allowing the situation to persist should form an integral part of your change plan.

You will need to develop strong resolve to see the process through, right up to termination of employment, if necessary. To do this, keeping your vision and the reason for implementing the change alive in your mind and heart will be tremendously helpful.

In addition, make sure to follow prudent steps such as:

- Securing your support.

- Allotting time in your calendar.

- Mastering the relevant policies and procedures.

- Documenting events meticulously.

- Using video-speak descriptions and the S-B-D feedback method.

- Maintaining your emotional equanimity.

- Taking care of yourself.

(continued)

REFLECTION

As you prepare to address the person whose behavior is chronically uncivil you may want to reflect on:

- What was management's role (your own and others) in enabling and possibly even encouraging the person's uncivil behavior?
- What specifically could or should have been done earlier to curb the uncivil behavior? What effect would that have had?
- What has prevented that from happening?
- Which of the factors that prevented effective action earlier are still present now? What might you do to mitigate these elements successfully?
- What was effective or partially effective in the past in dealing with this individual's behavior?
    - What got in the way of these initiatives being more effective?
    - Which elements of these initiatives might be useful to apply as you move forward now?
- What helpful factors, people or circumstances can you rely on now as you address the chronic behavior? In what ways?
- What is the first step you need to take now? The next step? The steps following that?
- How (specifically) will you take care of yourself as you go through this process?

IMPLEMENTATION CLINIC

Preparing for a Meeting with a Chronically Uncivil Team Member

Conversations to address chronically uncivil conduct require meticulous planning—the stakes are high, as are the chances of a strong and overt negative reaction that might involve a frontal attack on you personally.

As you prepare, consider these factors:

- What do you need to do before, during and after the meeting to maintain your calm?

- Who should you consult with prior to the meeting? What support and resources do you require?

- Does anyone else need to attend the meeting and if so, who? What type of advance joint planning is required?

- What materials do you need to review in advance (e.g., policies, collective agreement, previous documentation)?

- Considering the factors that could trigger a negative emotional reaction, where and when should the meeting take place?

- What (specifically) are your objectives for the meeting?

- What is your nonnegotiable, bottom-line outcome for the meeting?

- How will you begin the conversation? How will you frame the discussion and where will you go from there?

(continued)

- How will you ensure that the conversation remains on track? How will you handle derailments?

- What type of reactions can you anticipate? How will you handle strong emotional reactions that might come up, including attacks on you?

- What do you need to understand or learn during the meeting?

- How might you conclude the meeting? What type of summary will be most effective?

- What type of follow-up will you do to ensure that things remain on track (and what will you need to do in case things get off track)?

14

ACTION ON THE GROUND

KNOW EXACTLY WHAT TO SAY, HOW AND WHEN

....

CHOICES, CHOICES AND MORE CHOICES

As we return to the analogy of behaviors as screws and strategies as screwdrivers, how do you determine in any given situation what type of screw you are dealing with, and which screwdriver you should use? Should you respond on the spot, or later? Should you take a formal approach where you relay company expectations and policies, or should you take a gentle coaching angle?

There's a whole universe of screwdrivers out there, some of which you may be familiar with and have used, and others that you are completely unaware of. In this chapter we will analyze the full list of verbal choices at your disposal (some of which we have touched on in earlier parts of the book), and offer additional ones. To round it all up, we'll throw into the mix several options that you should remove from your toolkit altogether.

So, let's get down to work. What verbal options are available to you, no matter what situation you are faced with?

Table 11: Verbal Intervention Options

- Now or later
- Short or long
- In private or in public
- Formal/heavy or informal/light
- Big-picture statements
- "Here at …"
- "Let's not go there!"
- "We" frame
- S-B-D feedback
- Intervene-Switch

Now or Later?

Some situations require an immediate response. Other circumstances require a response later on. And some require both.

Responding on the spot offers several superb advantages. It sends a message in real time and, as such, leaves a lasting impact. If done the right way, things get resolved without much fuss and everyone can move forward, having had a useful teaching moment. And, in situations where the incivility took place in public, responding in the moment is often a must, as we discussed in chapter 11, Go Public.

In an ideal world, one would respond straightaway in most, if not all, cases. However, in real life, things are not always so simple. First, responding in the moment runs the risk of hitting the wrong note and, therefore, being ineffective or even damaging. Second, uncivil behaviors often happen very quickly and by the time you get your thoughts and actions together, the moment may have passed. Finally, many managers (and you might be one of them) do not trust their ability to intervene on the spot without inadvertently shaming the person whose behavior they are trying to correct.

The "respond later" option offers you the prospect of considering things carefully, perhaps even seeking additional input, and planning your intervention in more detail and with more subtlety. When you respond after the fact, you have the luxury of choosing the moment, location and even the people who you would include in whatever it is that you decide to do. On the other hand, the potential downfall of this option is that it can make the problem seem larger than it actually was in the moment.

You can use a combined in-the-moment and later option when the behavior was sufficiently serious for you to want to reinforce the message. You might respond in the moment with, say, a quick, "Folks, we're about to cross the line. Let's not go there!" and then engage in dialogue later with those who attended to discuss what happened and how it can be prevented from happening again. You could also add another "later" option whereby in a subsequent team meeting you discuss the importance of living the organizational values and describe behaviors that are incongruent with these values.

Short or Long?

There are many advantages to choosing a short response. A few well-chosen words can be very effective in getting a point across. Being succinct certainly curtails your own anxiety and conflict-avoidance tendencies from taking over and making you go on and on in circles, regretting the moment you ever opened your mouth in the first place. Keeping comments to a bare minimum is especially useful when the uncivil behavior was not severe or was clearly done without bad intent or awareness of its impact. In those situations, a long response would be unnecessary and could be perceived as harsh or odd.

A long response, on the other hand, allows you to include more details and offer more depth. Here you can incorporate an explanation as to why the behavior is unwelcome, or a reference to larger organizational values or a suggested path for action that would be different from the uncivil one. (You might recall examples of short and long responses from chapter 10, where in the section "Pulling the S-B-D Feedback Together" I showed how to use that structure to deliver effective messages of varying lengths.)

In Private or in Public?

Responding in private to address incivility is a great go-to strategy. When you do so, the world of options is endless. You can choose whether you will use an informal tone or a formal one, whether to keep it short or long, and the degree to which you want to engage in discourse about the matter. A private response offers you the opportunity to gain insight into the causes of the behavior, the employee's awareness of why the behavior is not welcome and the degree of openness to change that he or she possesses.

On the other hand, if you've read chapter 10, "Going Public," you know that sometimes the preferred way to deal with incivility is in public. This option is highly desirable when the bad behavior takes place in front of colleagues or clients—my rule of thumb is that what is done in public needs to be corrected on the spot and in public. Keep it as short as possible, intervene and move on immediately. The longer you linger, the greater the danger of the situation going south in a hurry.

A public forum (such as a meeting) is useful when your goal is to encourage conversation and dialogue about the issue. Other times, you may want to use this option to make a statement or explain the organization's position without necessarily getting into dialogue. For example, at an all-staff meeting you might want to reiterate that your organization does not accept employees speaking a foreign language on its premises. You could relay that there have been some instances of this lately and that you invite all staff to be mindful of this matter and help each other keep to the organization's formal language policy. You could add that you have already called some people's attention to this in private, and will continue to do so, emphasizing that repeat behaviors will not be accepted.

Light or Heavy? Formal or Informal?

Whether you consciously plan for it or not, your tone and demeanor will fall somewhere along the continuum between an informal, light approach and a more formal (or heavy-handed) one. In situations where the person clearly did not intend harm or was unaware of the effect of their actions, the light-handed approach would be most appropriate.

Generally, a heavy approach should be reserved for situations where the uncivil behavior is persistent, or where a one-time occurrence has crossed the line to such an extent that you need to impress upon the person the seriousness and inappropriateness of the behavior. For example, a situation where one person snorts loudly at a colleague's comment while adding, "I can't believe let you work here for so long" would warrant a more heavy-handed managerial response. You might say, "This comment and your body language are totally unacceptable and will not be tolerated. It violates our code of conduct and our team norms. I expect to never again see this type of behavior." Indeed, when you choose to go with a heavy-handed approach, you might go as far as citing the company policies, such as a code of conduct or a respect-in-the-workplace policy.

Big-Picture Statements

Use big-picture statements to refer to the larger values, beliefs or norms that your organization aspires to exhibit. If your organization believes in respect, collaboration, civility, teamwork or similar values, you have the option of referring to these as you intervene to boost civility and respect.

Referencing these overarching values frames the issue in its larger context and provides an indisputable rationale for the need to refrain from uncivil behavior. It also demonstrates your personal commitment to these principles. Furthermore, when framed in this way, it is very difficult for anyone to question your motivations or actions.

Over the course of hundreds of workshops, I have developed a particular affinity for referring to the bigger picture using the phrase "Here at…" Through continuous experimentation and the feedback that I receive, I have learned that this simple phrasing is easy for leaders to adopt. Starting your corrective intervention with this expression seems to feel natural and authentic to those speaking and to those listening, and most leaders I work with embrace it instantaneously as a strategy they can use in real life. Here's how it might sound:

- *"Here at Mountainous University, we believe in diversity."*
- *"Here at the Emergency Department, collaborative teamwork is part of who we are."*
- *"Here at UVN, we pride ourselves on the respect we demonstrate in all our actions."*

Starting your communication with a big-picture statement such as "Here at …" helps you remember and remain connected to the reason for your intervention and reminds you of your resolve to create a civil work environment.

"Let's Not Go There"

By now, you have encountered the words "Let's not go there" in numerous places in this book. This little phrase helps you respond constructively in a surprisingly wide range of situations. It is highly effective in sending a clear stop message without relying too heavily on your institutional power. And it assumes that people will intuitively grasp that a line has been crossed and why.

Because of the way this phrase is structured, it reduces the probability of the offender getting unnecessarily defensive. No shaming or blaming—it allows everyone involved to save face. Furthermore, the nice thing about it is that you'll be able to recall this phrase easily anytime you really need it, because it comprises only four simple words. It is simple, simple, and did I say—simple.

When you have no better words, "Let's not go there" will certainly do. That alone makes it a great "now" strategy. And you can make it light or heavy by using different pitches (high? low?), or emphasizing different words ("Let's not go *there*" will sound different from "Let's *not* go there"). You can be quick as lightning, or slow as molasses, light-hearted or dead-serious ... you get the idea.

You can use "Let's not go there" before or after other statements as necessary. For example:

- *"Criticizing a colleague in front of a client is unacceptable. Let's not go there."*
- *"Let's not go there—these comments don't fit with our team norms."*

Consider sharing this phrase with your team members as a joint strategy that will help them effectively (and respectfully) hold each other accountable and halt unprofessional behavior as it occurs in real time. This simple expression is sure to do the job.

"We" Frame

You must always beware of inadvertently laying blame or landing on a heavier note than you had intended. If you are irritated or upset with the person, this sentiment is likely going to ooze through into your words and actions. Your intention might be to be fair and measured, but your voice and tone will send a very different message. The person at the receiving end of your message might get upset, offended or humiliated. That is clearly not the result you are after.

This is where using the "we" frame comes in handy. Inserting phrases such as "we," "let's," "let's not," "us," "our," "together," "all" or "all of us," reduces the potential for a tone of blame—it softens your communication. Essentially, using this frame suggests that you understand that we are all humans who sometimes make mistakes, that everyone is in the same boat at one point or another, and that you are supportive as you walk alongside your people on the trial-and-error path for growth, trying to do your best.

Here are some examples of "we" framing in action:

- *"Let's make sure that we demonstrate respect for each other's opinions."*
- *"In this hospital, we speak only English while on shift."*
- *"We all need to alert the meeting convener when we know we might be arriving late."*

S-B-D Feedback

Chapter 10 described the S-B-D feedback method in great detail and outlined how it can serve you in numerous situations. Whether in public or in private, short or long, serious or light, relying on a solid structure that you can adapt to the circumstances will allow you to respond in what sometimes are very challenging circumstances—you will deliver a message that is clear and constructive, feeling confident as you do so.

The Intervene-Switch Move

You may recall this strategy from the earlier discussion in chapter 11 about objectives and considerations when you go public. Essentially, the Intervene-Switch refers to you changing the topic of conversation into a neutral one immediately after correcting someone's behavior. In chapter 11, I highly recommended using this tactic as part of any intervention that takes place in public, because it offers an easy escape for all who are present from the unpleasant moment when you comment on an undesirable behavior.

Intervene-Switch might sound like this:

"I want to remind everyone that making hissing noises when you don't like what someone is suggesting is not okay. Now, moving on, does anyone happen to know whether they announced which movies are up for the Oscars?"

MIXING AND MATCHING VERBAL INTERVENTIONS

As you can see, no matter what response you choose, it will mesh together some combination of the strategies above, whether or not you are able to articulate exactly which ones you selected and why.

Each situation requires a different set of metaphorical screwdrivers. In one situation you might intervene using a short + informal + public constellation, whereas in another instance you'll choose long + private + heavy. As you reflect on situations that you have dealt with, you may realize that in some of these you used a winning combination that yielded great results. In other instances you may have selected the wrong mix and then were disappointed with the outcome. It's quite possible that you employed a heavy touch where a light touch would have sufficed, or opted for a delayed response where an immediate one would have been more appropriate.

I highly recommend that you take the time to reflect on your past interventions (as well as those that you will undertake in the future) and analyze in detail (as above) which strategies and combinations you used, and the impact that your choices had on the final outcome. There is a strong likelihood you will discover that you tend to use the same combinations over and over because they are the ones with which you are most comfortable. But as you have learned in this chapter, there may be other strategies and combinations that would work far better in certain circumstances than your usual go-to interventions. The more you are aware of what strategies you are choosing, and how effective or ineffective they are in specific circumstances, the better you will become at handling these tricky situations.

In the Implementation Clinic at the end of this chapter, you will find three cases for your review. Try to see whether you can analyze correctly which strategies were used in each of these cases.

VERBAL RESPONSES TO AVOID

Let's look at another example of a situation that happens in public, to illustrate some of the minefields you might encounter, and things you should avoid doing. Imagine this:

You work as a recruitment supervisor in a large healthcare institution. You love your job because you get to interview and hire bright-eyed nurses with promising futures who bring to the organization new ideas and innovative methods.

Action on the Ground | 249

One day, running between meetings with five minutes to spare, you drop over to the coffee shop to grab a coffee. You're wearing a badge that clearly identifies you as a manager.

There's a patient in a wheelchair at the head of the line, followed by four people who seem to be sharing a casual conversation. Of the four, two are staff who report directly to you.

As you stand there waiting for your turn, one of the people who report to you (a veteran who prides herself on being an avid advocate for optimal patient care) says in a voice loud enough for everyone in line to hear, "I can't believe how the nursing standards around here have deteriorated! They hire all these young nurses with no real-life experience, and of course you get what you pay for. I wonder when that new generation will ever learn how to do things properly. As far as I can tell, they're all pretty useless."

What (specifically) would you say or do in this situation?

If you are like many of the managers I've worked with over the years, you'd probably feel like a deer caught in the headlights if faced with a situation like this. A million thoughts run through your mind simultaneously. Your inner canary's intense response demands your attention. With your manager badge scorching into your chest, you know there are so many things that you could say or do, but you are paralyzed by the fear of doing it wrong, with potentially horrible ramifications.

So let's make sure that of the many options you consider, you avoid taking those that are better avoided altogether. As you reflect on past experiences where you had to respond in the moment to incivility, you will probably find that you used one or all of the strategies below:

- Humor
- Sarcasm
- I-messages
- Educating the person by disputing the content of what they said
- Showing displeasure through disapproving sounds, facial expressions or physical gestures

On the face of it, each of these responses seems to have merit, which is why so many managers use them at their moment of need. However, as you will see momentarily, upon closer examination it becomes readily apparent that none of these interventions is useful. In fact, they will invariably take you down dangerous paths that lead to undesirable destinations.

Humor

Humor is a wonderful thing. It is a great connector. It brings lightness to uncomfortable situations. It relieves interpersonal tension. It is a great tool that leaders can use in many situations. However, when it comes to correcting behavior, humor is, in almost all situations, a risky choice.

Unless you are one of those rare people who are blessed with the gift of a sense of humor that never hits the wrong note, using humor to deal with incivility is highly problematic. Chances are that what you think is funny will be perceived by the person at the receiving end as offensive or inappropriate. If you reflect on your own experiences using humor, you will probably find more than one example where you saw the words leaving your mouth, just like in one of those old cartoons where the spoken words come out of the character's mouth as if they were written on a banner, and no effort in the world can reel them back and right up into your head so that you can pretend that they never left your lips in the first place.

Furthermore, when you use humor to correct behavior, there's a very high chance that the seriousness of your message will be lost. As you saw earlier in this chapter, a light touch (conveyed through a relaxed body posture, a friendly rather than stern facial expression and a light tone of voice) still communicates that the behavior needs to stop and is, therefore, often the best path to take. Humor, on the other hand, does not necessarily create the same effect successfully. I therefore suggest that you reserve your humor to low-risk situations and avoid using it to correct behavior.

In the coffee-shop case described above, a humorous response (if you were able to come up with one) would most likely hit the wrong note. It would also send a message to your staff, to the patient in the wheelchair and to the two other people in line that speaking disparagingly and openly about a specific group (younger-generation nurses) is not taken seriously. That it is a matter to laugh about, with no real consequences. A broken window that no one cares to fix. This is definitely not the message you would want to convey.

In this situation, the combination of the following "screwdrivers" would be a good, effective choice: now, light touch, in public, short, *Let's not go there,* and intervene-switch. It could sound something like:

"Excuse me for interrupting. I happened to hear the conversation about young nurses—it doesn't reflect our inclusive culture. Let's not go there. Now, has anyone tried those cranberry muffins? They look pretty awesome."

Sarcasm

Are you ready for one of our little "50–50 deal," tête-à-tête moments? If you consider yourself to be someone who possesses a sarcastic personality, I'd like to remind you (yes, especially you) that our little deal consists of me committing to be opinionated and you committing to considering these opinions with an open mind. Are you ready?

Sarcasm is a practice that leaders should remove from their behavioral lexicon entirely. It is a backhanded way to deliver a message that people use when they are afraid of dealing with others directly and honestly. It renders those on the receiving end helpless to respond. It engenders resentment, anger and even rage in those at whom it is directed. It creates an unpleasant environment for everyone. It reflects poorly on you as a leader and diminishes the respect that people may otherwise have toward you. It erodes goodwill in others, especially those who are its direct subjects.

Even more, sarcasm does not send a clear message about what specifically you want changed. From a leadership perspective, it does not provide the guidance that you should offer. Instead, it sends a debilitating and punitive response and it usually does not provide specific information about which behaviors are inappropriate or why. For example, in the hospital coffee-shop scenario, a sarcastic comment such as "That's exactly the kind of open-minded conversation I love hearing when I'm waiting in line" seems more like a rebuke of a child than a mature comment directed at adults.

Furthermore, the sarcastic comment would likely be offensive to the person whose behavior you are remarking on, and that itself constitutes incivility. Instead, what you should be doing is using a light touch that still sends a clear stop message (as suggested above in the "humor" section). Or you could choose to be more serious and say specifically that conversations distinguishing people based on the group they belong to are unacceptable in your hospital, or that comments that degrade other people's skills or expertise are not welcome in your environment.

I-Messages

Coined by psychologist Thomas Gordon in the 1960s, the term "I-message" (or "I-statement") refers to a method of conveying a message in an assertive fashion, without putting the listener on the defensive. (We touched on these messages earlier on, as part of the discussion in chapter 11 about responding in public.) When you use an I-message, you take ownership of your feelings rather than blaming the other person for your reactions. In what he termed as "confrontive" I-messages, you begin by describing the other person's behavior, then outline its effect on you and your feelings about it. As in, "When you tell me that there's no time left on the agenda to discuss my idea, I feel that my contribution isn't valued." I-messages have become the gold standard for assertive communication and are widely held in high regard as a constructive means of respectful communication.

Indeed, I-messages are a very effective communication strategy in many situations, but not for correcting uncivil behavior.

In my workplace incivility training sessions for managers, I set up a case study similar to the coffee-shop scenario described in this chapter and ask managers to brainstorm best ways to respond to this situation. Not surprisingly, they very often suggest using some variation of I-messaging, along the lines of the statement, "I am offended by your comments."

When this happens, I challenge my participants to delete I-messages from their vocabulary whenever they have to correct behavior. There is a time and a place for a manager to use I-messages (and we will examine these instances in the next chapter when we discuss incivility directed at you personally), but not when you are attempting to give feedback to an employee who is behaving in an uncivil fashion. Here's why: It's not about you or your feelings or your personal upset. The reason you are intervening is because the behavior contradicts the company values or your team's aspirations. Your personal feelings have nothing to do with it, and bringing them into the picture just muddies things up. It introduces a subjective element that turns the matter into a personal issue between you and the individual who made the remark, instead of being a general comment about what is accepted or unaccepted in your workplace, on your watch.

Educating, or Disputing the Content

In the hospital coffee-shop scenario, you might feel an irresistible urge to contest the accuracy of the comment that the person has just made. After all, as the person responsible for recruiting those talented young nurses, you have firsthand understanding of the tremendous advantages that they bring to the organization. You know for a fact that the disparaging statements about these young nurses are utterly misinformed and inaccurate. You are upset that these comments were made in public and concerned that they will create the impression that they are valid. You see it as your responsibility to ensure that everyone, including the patient in the wheelchair, can trust that nurses of any age in your hospital adhere to the highest professional standards.

And yet, a word of caution. There are two compelling reasons that should prevent you from disputing the content of remarks such as these, or attempting to quasi-educate the person about the inaccuracy of their perception.

The first reason echoes the rationale that I used to discourage you from using I-messages. That is, the main problem with the critical remarks is not their content. Rather, the main issue is that conversations that are uncivil or degrade others are not to be had on your company premises. If you stick to this approach across your interventions, people will eventually understand that it's not about this group or another, or about a particular rude gesture or expression, it is about the fact that such behaviors are incongruent with your desired culture in the first place.

Second, on a practical level, trying to educate the individual or dispute the content might get you personally into a compromised situation, as well as deteriorate the conversation into even more unacceptable places. To illustrate, here's a typical scenario that could unfold in this case, once you attempt to educate or dispute the content:

Speaker: *"I can't believe how the nursing standards around here have deteriorated! They hire all these young nurses with no real-life experience, and of course you get what you pay for. I wonder when that new generation will ever learn how to do things properly. As far as I can tell, they're all pretty useless."*

You: *"I'm sorry, I couldn't help overhearing your remark. As a manager and the person responsible for recruiting new hires, I feel obliged to comment. I can tell you that the young nurses bring to our organization up-to-date skills and new information that feed our drive for excellence. I am very proud of the fact that our hospital has been making a concerted effort to hire as many of these nurses as possible, and I can assure you that they make a great contribution."*

Speaker: *"Well, I don't mean to be disrespectful to your work, but to be honest, you need to know that maybe these girls do a great job in making a good impression when they're interviewing for the position, but once they land the job and get that regular paycheck, I can tell you firsthand that they show a very different side of themselves. They're lazy and they're not willing to put in the hard work that nurses like us used to do in the old days and, frankly, still do. These girls and boys think they know everything and don't listen to what people like me have learned through years of real-life experience. Perhaps the recruiters should come into the wards to see what all those fancy-schmancy recruits are really like six months or a year after they've been hired!"*

As you can see, this conversation has deteriorated within seconds of you trying to defend the inaccuracy of the comments. You chose the option of educating, and decreased the chances of success further by electing to use the "long" screwdriver instead of the "short" one (which is usually the preferred choice whenever you respond to uncivil behavior in public). There is no good way to get out of this blunder. So my recommendation is that you just don't go there in the first place.

Disapproving Sounds, Facial Expressions or Body Language

"After attending this session I think I'll have to stop the sounds I use when I hear my staff becoming rowdy and noisy in the corridor just outside my office. I come out of my office, stand by the door and make this loud 'tssss' sound to get their attention and indicate that they should tone it down. I thought this was more respectful than making a verbal comment that others might hear, but now I realize that I'm treating them as if they were stray cats, and that my own reaction is just as uncivil as their behavior."

—*Relayed in the course of a Workplace Incivility for Leaders training session by a call center manager*

Many leaders use verbal sounds and body gestures to curtail behavior of which they disapprove. In some of our workplace incivility sessions, I get participants to demonstrate what type of body gestures or facial expressions they have used to deal with bad behavior in the moment that it occurs. The wide range (and hilariousness) of the behaviors generates roars of laughter as everyone realizes how ridiculous and uncivil these attempts are. I have heard the oddest sounds, and seen hugely expressive hand gestures, turned backs, eyebrows raised with exaggerated surprise, noses crunched with disgust, lips pursed as if they had just come in contact with a sour lemon. You name it, and some leader has used it somewhere, sometime, in a futile attempt to stop incivility in its tracks.

So let's forget about the dismissive sounds, facial expressions and body language. They will not achieve their purpose. They may be perceived as uncivil and rude themselves (which they often are). They are a poor attempt at escaping your responsibility as a leader to act in a direct and honest way. Instead, follow the sage advice that teachers often offer to the children in their care: Use your words.

IMPLEMENTATION CLINIC

What to Say, When and How

Your verbal intervention options include:

- Now or later
- Short or long
- In private or in public
- Formal/heavy or informal/light
- Big-picture statements
- "Here at..."
- "Let's not go there!"
- "We" frame
- S-B-D feedback
- Intervene-Switch

And you should avoid:

- Humor
- Sarcasm
- I-messages
- Educating the person by disputing the content of what they said
- Showing displeasure through disapproving sounds, facial expressions or physical gestures

Analyzing the interventions below, can you tell which of the strategies discussed in this chapter the leader used in each case?

Case No. 1

"This type of banter can make people feel uncomfortable. It doesn't fit with the type of inclusive environment we believe in, so let's just cut it out."

Strategies used were:

1. _____

2. _____

3. _____

4. _____

5. _____

Case No. 2

"Yesterday I heard an exchange among several team members who were bantering about telling 'husband and wife' jokes. Everyone was laughing, and the jokes were probably very funny. I'm commenting on this to the whole team because it doesn't really matter who specifically engaged in these jokes. The point is that any jokes that stereotype people create an environment where it's all right to laugh at the expense of other groups. This type of atmosphere affects people in all kinds of negative ways, even if they don't belong to the group that's being discussed. It ends up creating a poisoned environment. It certainly doesn't fit with our core values. The company, as well as myself personally, expect that we use humor in ways that don't demean other groups or people, regardless of whether or not anyone in the room seems upset about it."

(continued)

Strategies used were:

1. _____

2. _____

3. _____

4. _____

5. _____

Case No. 3

"Here at Earthbound, we value collaboration. Telling someone to go find someone else to help them doesn't fit with that. Please help Gerry as he requested. Now, has anyone seen the latest call-in report data?"

Strategies used were:

1. _____

2. _____

3. _____

4. _____

5. _____

Answers

Case 1: big picture, short, light, now, "we" frame

Case 2: long, public, later, formal/heavy, big picture

Case 3: big picture, S-B-D feedback, now, short, light, intervene-switch

15

DEALING WITH INCIVILITY THAT IS DIRECTED TOWARD YOU

....

Up to now, we've discussed situations where workplace incivility takes place between staff members and you, as a manager, have to confront them to tame it. But just like anyone else, you too might be subject to incivility. Your feelings might be hurt, you might find yourself in Velcro-land and you will occasionally feel like getting even. Typically, incivility will be directed at you from one or more of several sources: a colleague, an employee, your manager or a union representative. Each of these requires a different approach.

INCIVILITY FROM COLLEAGUES

When a colleague treats you in uncivil ways, the first thing to do is decide whether or not you will take the matter to heart. People can say things in the heat of the moment, or be rude when they are under pressure, or exclude you with no bad intentions. Or possibly they are unaware that their behavior is uncivil or that it is impacting you negatively. Giving your colleagues some leeway, understanding and forgiveness and then moving on is an excellent strategy in many instances. After all, wouldn't you want to receive the same generosity from them when you make a mistake?

Sometimes, however, uncivil behavior reflects a deeper issue that might need addressing. Your colleague might have difficulties with you or is frustrated by things you do or say. In this case, it is important to open a dialogue about what is really going on and to keep an open mind and heart to their issues and feedback without getting defensive. Your goal should always be to have collegial and productive relationships with your fellow managers.

If you decide to address a matter that affected you negatively, consider using two of the strategies that in the previous chapter I strongly discouraged you from using when you are addressing employee incivility: humor and I-messages. In the case of taming incivility with your own employees, as their manager, the emphasis is on setting the standard and owning your leadership role. But dealing with a peer has more to do with you as a person and you have less of a responsibility to act from a place of obligation to implement the organizational messages.

Using humor will lighten the situation and put a positive spin on it while still indicating that you do not want to be treated that way. It sends the message that you are not going to make a huge deal of the issue and that your attitude is both practical and forgiving. Your colleague will appreciate this approach and in all likelihood will change course.

To address the situation using I-messages, use my B-A-R structure. In essence, you communicate with your colleague using a three-point message:

1. **Behavior:** Orient the person to the behavior and situation (or situations) that affected you:
   - Describe the facts: who, when, where, what
   - Use observable terms, no amateur diagnosis or speculation

2. **Affect:** Describe how your colleague's behavior affected you in the following spheres:

- Your feelings or experience
  and/or
- Factual impact, consequences

3. **Request:** Describe what you'd like to happen next time or what might work better, or communicate a clear "stop."

Here's how the B-A-R formula might sound:

"Frank, our relationship is important to me and I want to make sure that we work really well together on this project. There's something that's been nagging at me that I'd like to talk to you about. Do you have a moment?

"Yesterday morning, when we were standing by your desk and talking about the upcoming cuts, I suggested that we try using another software that I used to use in my previous job to save on operational costs. You said that people were tired of hearing about how good things were in my other job and how great I was, and that I should get with the program. I take responsibility for not having explained my idea in sufficient detail in the first place and realize that you had no intention of offending or upsetting me. Still, I felt upset by these comments and am also concerned that an opportunity to create savings might be missed. If you have an issue with things I do, I want to hear about it and respond, which is harder for me to do when I experience the comments as harsh. Please let me know what's on your mind in a supportive way. Will that work for you?"

Notice that the feedback included two of the earlier tactics that I recommended using when providing corrective S-B-D feedback: owning your contribution ("I take responsibility for not having explained my idea") and assigning benevolent intent ("I realize that you had no intention of offending or upsetting").

Remember to begin with an introductory comment that frames the conversation in a larger positive context and highlights constructive intentions, such as in the example above, and end by opening an opportunity for dialogue.

INCIVILITY FROM STAFF

You're in a meeting in your office with one of your staff members. This person is a veteran employee with strong opinions about anything and everything. You outline the details of a new project that the department has been charged with, and the specific tasks that this employee will need to take on as part of this new project.

Judging by facial expressions and body language, the information does not sit well with the employee. When you are done with the explanation and invite the person to offer feedback, he responds with an agitated tone and slightly raised voice, "I can't believe you're asking someone with my experience to do this kind of stuff. It's demeaning." Pointing a finger straight at you he adds, "And you and the rest of them should know better!" He then gets up and leaves the room, slamming the door behind him.

How would you respond to this situation?

I have heard surprising and sometimes disturbing stories from managers about uncivil behavior that is directed at them by people who report to them. As I see it, when employees permit themselves to be openly hostile toward a person in authority (where they could suffer serious consequences), they are likely already behaving in similar ways toward colleagues as well, thereby poisoning the work environment. The behavior toward you is a symptom of a bigger problem, and you should treat it as such.

The single most important thing to do is not get personally triggered when this happens to you. No matter how upset you become, hold on at all times to the notion that you are the manager, whose job it is to maintain emotional equanimity while also ensuring that the work environment is respectful and the organizational values are lived out. Do not succumb to the temptation to make it about you, such as telling the person that you personally were upset by the comment and asking that they apologize to you.

Instead, keep your response firmly couched within the larger picture. The S-B-D feedback method will serve you well in this instance. I recommend leaving your own feelings out of it altogether, but if you wish to insert your personal reaction into the mix, do so in a secondary and nonemotional fashion.

Your follow-up with this employee might sound like this (reference to your personal reaction appears in parentheses):

"Here at Elora's, the expectation is that we treat each other with respect even when we are upset or disagree. Behaviors such as pointing fingers, shutting doors with force and telling a manager that they should know better, as you just did, do not fit with this standard. (Frankly, it can also be personally upsetting to the person at the receiving end of this behavior.) The expectation moving forward is that you refrain from such behaviors and instead express your reservations verbally, and in a constructive fashion."

Once you have clearly outlined the expectation moving forward, if the person continues to exhibit uncivil behaviors, especially if he or she repeats the original conduct, you will need to take the matter more seriously, just as you would any other situation where an employee continues to behave in undesirable ways despite your intervention. Again, refrain from taking it personally or making it about you. This is about the civility of the environment and creating a workplace where everyone can perform at their best. So do what you need to do to protect the integrity of the work environment, including escalating the issue to a performance management level.

INCIVILITY FROM YOUR MANAGER

When your own manager is uncivil toward you, the power differential between you will play an important role in determining how you should best respond. The risks are different, and possibly higher, than when you respond to a colleague's or employee's uncivil behavior. Your approach will also be influenced by whether the manager is chronically uncivil toward you, or whether it is an infrequent, and maybe even rare, occurrence.

When I conduct my civility-boosting training sessions for leaders, I invite everyone to brainstorm and come up with a joint list of uncivil behaviors. We then examine the list together and reflect on its meaning. Then, I add a little twist: I ask for a show of hands from everyone who has demonstrated at least two or three of the listed behaviors in the past several days. Without exception, and regardless of the size of the group, all hands are raised.

This repeated reaction demonstrates not only that we are all human, but that we engage regularly in counterproductive behaviors and habits without pausing to consider seriously their possible impact on others. This applies to the way you conduct yourself with the people who report to you, and it equally applies to the way your manager behaves with you.

So what works when it is your manager who is being uncivil to you? You may wish to try any or all of the ideas below. Check out the next Implementation Clinic for additional ones.

- **Extend the benefit of the doubt.** The best place to begin is by assuming that your manager intends no harm, and that the impact of his or her behavior is lodged in their blind spot. Adopting this approach will make it more possible for you to develop a Teflon skin and not take things to heart. Furthermore, if you do decide to raise the matter with your manager, then extending the benefit of the doubt will lessen the chances that your stress, resentment and victimhood will inadvertently leak into the conversation. And, of course, you will want to verbally express your assumption that your boss's motives are essentially benevolent. You might say things such as:

  - *"My sense is that when you made the comment about my report being late, you were speaking out of frustration, and without intending to upset me or dismiss my work."*
    or
  - *"I know you are under so much stress with the new project and I can appreciate that the little niceties can sometimes get lost in the shuffle when the pressure is so high."*

- **Speak up.** Muster the courage to speak up constructively. In all likelihood, raising the issue in a well-thought-out way will be appreciated and will lead to positive change. Avoid blame, which will trigger unnecessary defensiveness. Talk about the effects of the behavior on you, on your people or on the work you do, using "I" rather than "you" language, since the latter can unintentionally trigger defensiveness. Don't come across as a victim or a whiner. Most importantly, maintain a calm and open demeanor through your tone and body language.

  Once you decide to address the matter with your manager, you will need to think carefully about your strategy. You will likely want to strive for the following objectives:

1. Maintain the relationship.
2. Honor your own experience, and theirs.
3. Communicate clearly which behaviors are of concern.
4. Clarify what you'd like to see happen.
5. Trigger positive change.

Plan in advance what you will say. Whether you intend to set aside a particular time to discuss the matter, or whether you are devising a response that you will use in the moment when your manager repeats the behavior, consider carefully what phrases you should use. Your goal is to be productive and help your manager change his or her behavior, not to make things worse. The B-A-R structure discussed earlier will work in this instance very well. It offers you a solid structure you can rely on, especially if you open with a constructive comment.

If your manager is chronically uncivil or even abrasive, carefully considering every detail of your approach is all the more important. You may be very successful in helping them to change this behavior, even surprisingly so.

- **Set boundaries.** Gracefully set clear boundaries related to what's okay and not okay with you. You can do so in an organic way, such that you deal with one situation at a time, on the spot or shortly thereafter. In this case, you can use a serious approach, or a light or humorous one, but make sure that the "stop" message comes across clearly. It might be as simple as saying, "I am open to critical feedback—it helps me improve. When this type of feedback is conveyed to me in front of others, it is harder for me to respond constructively. I would really appreciate having these types of conversations in private."

You can also utilize a more formal approach, setting a special time to speak about the matters that are on your mind, or use already-existing opportunities such as performance appraisals, regular supervision times or progress meetings.

- **Self-care.** Take good care of yourself, because, when all is said and done, you are all that you've got. Do whatever you need to do for stress relief, both at work and at home. Simple stress-relieving strategies that will calm down your fight-or-flight reaction can be surprisingly helpful, including deep diaphragmatic breathing, taking a short break or talking to someone you trust who will help you gain perspective. Do whatever you know works for you to protect your resilience and equanimity.

- **Develop your Teflon shield.** Replace your Velcro reaction with a Teflon-inspired attitude so that you can allow things to slide right off you. There really is no need to take everything to heart. Simple self-talk can do wonders in this regard. Try using thinking mantras, such as "He doesn't really mean it," "This too shall pass," "Don't sweat the small stuff" or "It's only a job."

- **Mind your own mental business.** Remain mentally in your own business rather than meddling in theirs. Byron Katie, whose work has transformed the lives of people around the world, asserts that much of our suffering occurs when we mentally obsess over things that are not in our control but rather are someone else's mental business, in that they are under their domain and control.[30] When you are upset and your mind is filled with thoughts about what your manager should or should not be doing, you are mentally immersed in your manager's business rather than your own. To unhook yourself in the midst of upset and Velcro reactions, pause for a brief moment and ask yourself this question: "Whose business am I in right now, when

I am believing the thought that my boss should treat me with more respect? Am I mentally in her business or mine?" (Hint: Whenever you think that someone else should or should not do something, you are in their business, not yours, because only she or he has control over what they do.)

- **Free your mind.** Remind yourself that this is just a job and that you have the option to leave anytime you want to. When you find yourself feeling anxious at the thought of leaving your current role because you are too old, or the pension is too good, or the market is too small—you get my drift—remind yourself (literally, say it out loud to yourself, or speak it loudly in your mind, or do some journaling) that you will always have options, even if sometimes it doesn't seem that way.

- **Work the system.** Take the issue to someone who has influence. If you're lucky, your organization might already have processes and internal resources designed to support people in your situation. If not, you'll need to figure out a way to use internal resources in an informal fashion to trigger some helpful change. You will need to be thoughtful and savvy, as you do not want to jeopardize your relationship with your boss, who might naturally be upset if you go to others before approaching him or her.

But what if, you may ask, despite your best efforts, nothing changes and your boss remains uncivil or even abrasive? Well, then, it might be high time to polish the dust off your résumé and go find a better place, where you can safely (and happily) park your talent, body and soul.

INCIVILITY FROM A UNION REPRESENTATIVE

Sometimes it is difficult to draw the distinction between strong opinions that are expressed legitimately as part of labor relations activities, and actions that cross the line of respect and civility. I have worked with union representatives who felt that management was dictatorial and closed-minded to the extent that the only way to get them to listen was through actions and even insult. And I have seen stressed-out managers whose dark-circled eyes bore testament to sleepless nights caused by strife with a union representative, situations where persistent incivility from union leaders led to managers' stress leave and, in one memorable case, even early retirement. In these cases, managers felt helpless to protect themselves because they were told by their own managers that any action on their part to curb the union steward's abrasiveness would trigger labor unrest and, therefore, they were to ignore the behavior. In essence, they were left to fend for themselves and advised to acquire thicker skins.

To determine whether or not the behavior that is directed at you by a union member is civil, let's go back to our Raise the Banner strategy (chapter 8). Can the words or actions directed at you by the union representative be hung above the company's front entrance? Can they form part of the banner that lets the world know what happens in your establishment behind closed doors? If the answer is yes, these types of words or deeds are to be expected within any reasonable work environment, you will need to accept what is happening and move on. However, if posting those behaviors on the banner would be problematic, then these behaviors must cease. You have the right to demand that your employer protect you from this uncivil conduct. This is not a situation that you should handle on your own, because the stakes are high and the complexities too great. You need to go to your own manager, or as high in the hierarchy as it takes, and advocate that you, like any other employee, have the right to work in a respectful, psychologically safe work environment.

HAVING TAKEN A LOOK at the situations in which you personally might be subject to incivility and how you can address these situations, check out this chapter's Implementation Clinic for additional practical ideas. Then, let's meet up at the final chapter of the book, where we will think together about the best ways of putting it all together—putting all that you have learned into action.

IMPLEMENTATION CLINIC

When Incivility Is Directed at You

When incivility is directed at you, take action. It might come your way from a colleague, someone who reports to you, your own manager or a union representative who is overstepping his or her legitimate role. Each of these situations bears unique risks and, therefore, should be handled differently.

Reflect on your experiences since you first took on a leadership role and consider the following.

Have you ever been treated in an uncivil fashion by:

- A colleague?

- Someone who reported to you?

- Your manager?

- A union representative?

- In each of these situations, what action did you take?

- On a scale of 1 to 10, with 10 meaning "highly effective" and 1 being "highly ineffective," how would you rate the effectiveness of your response in each case?

- What would have made your response(s) more effective?

- Based on your experiences thus far, and on the strategies outlined in this chapter, what would you do differently next time?

IMPLEMENTATION CLINIC

Giving Feedback to Your Uncivil Boss

If you decide to go ahead and provide feedback to a manager who demonstrates incivility, consider doing the following:

- Choose the forum carefully (a regular meeting or one that's specially convened?) and place your item strategically on the agenda (first item? middle? last?). Avoid email.

- If you're in the same physical location, meet face-to-face. If you're in different locations, choose the best semi-personal medium available.

- Assess in advance how ready your manager is to hear the message. He or she may not be open to it and defensiveness might ensue. If so, consider even more carefully the circumstances and the wording of your message.

- Tailor your communication to his or her specific listening frequencies. Listening is not a linear event; in fact, it's a highly subjective process that is informed by the listener's worldview, motivators, priorities, aspirations and fears. For your boss to be able to hear you, you'll need to transmit your message in a frequency they can hear. Ask yourself what drives, scares or inspires them, and then frame your message accordingly. For example, if your manager is motivated by a drive to help the organization become a sector leader, tell them that the behavior creates a fear of taking risks and, therefore, stifles innovation.

- As part of your preparation, put yourself in your manager's shoes and list any possible objections and concerns that might arise.

Craft your message in such a way that it addresses these objections well before the manager has a chance to raise them.

- Your boss is, in all likelihood, unaware of the negative impact that his or her behavior is having—it is lodged in their blind spot. You'll need to be very descriptive about the behaviors that are problematic and clearly outline the effects of these behaviors.

- Thoughtful planning regarding desirable words you should use, and words to avoid, will make or break the day. Certain words will trigger defensiveness and will lead to failure or even damage the relationship, whereas a good selection of words and phrases will pave the way for meaningful dialogue and subsequent change.

- Begin the discussion with a brief review of the big picture and context, and then switch to your key points. Lay out the facts in an organized fashion, zeroing in on what they need to know, in a way that they can hear.

- Tell it like it is. Candor will garner respect.

- Solutions, solutions, solutions! Stating a problem without offering viable solutions will derail matters in a hurry.

Dedicating time and effort to crafting your message carefully will pay off in spades. If you are unprepared, the cocktail of adrenaline, cortisol and anxiety in your blood might lead you to stumble.

Good luck!

16

MAKE IT HAPPEN
WHERE TO GO FROM HERE

....

PREPARATION, ACTION, SUCCESS

Now that you have added the information and strategies outlined in *Trust Your Canary* to your already-existing leadership arsenal of ideas, observations, experiences, mistakes, lessons learned and wisdom, let's turn our attention to what you will need to do to actually apply what you have learned to boost civility in the daily reality that you inhabit.

Let's face it: Change will not necessarily be easy, and it may not happen over a day, a month or even a year. But one step at a time, one situation at a time, you can do it!

Deal with Resistance

If you've ever tried to do something new and significant, you know that you will probably meet the formidable forces of resistance.

First and foremost is your own inner resistance. In fact, you (yes, you!) might prove be the most challenging force with which you will have to contend. For starters, see how many of the following thoughts and feelings apply to your thinking:

- I can't fight a culture that has been engrained for years.
- The task is too big.

- I'm not sure I care enough.
- It'll never work.
- No one before me ever succeeded.
- I'm too busy with more important things.
- I can't take on some of these people.
- I don't have the support I need.
- I don't have the necessary experience or skills.
- The timing is wrong.
- I wouldn't know where to start.
- I'm too stressed.

Look inward and deal with your limiting thoughts, beliefs and feelings, until you find the clarity you need and the resolve that will help propel you forward. (It might help if you remind yourself why you are doing this in the first place.) Once you work through your issues, you will be free to take meaningful action on the ground.

You will also need to make a firm commitment to walking the talk—modeling civility at all times, being open to feedback and apologizing when necessary. There is no point in initiating change if you personally are unable to embody it.

As you begin to change yourself and to reshape the work environment, you will likely encounter some forms of resistance from the team. If your team is of the Healthy Body or Persistent Allergy types (as described in chapter 1), then one can reasonably predict that you will encounter little problems, if any. Such resistance will likely emanate from the one person, or few people, who tend to be uncivil on a more persistent basis.

If, however, your team is in a Chronic Infection or Acute Disease state, then you might experience significant resistance. It will show up up in many forms, including direct challenges to your leadership or uncivil behaviors aimed at dismissing and belittling your efforts, character and intentions.

Accept this resistance as a natural by-product of any meaningful change—don't take it personally and don't let it slow you down. Instead, invest in increasing your sphere of influence, changing minds and winning people over. Remind yourself that people want to work in a respectful environment where they can perform at their best and that it is your responsibility (and privilege) to remove obstacles that might prevent them from doing so. You will need to hold firm with those who are chronically uncivil, which will require conviction, patience and stamina. Paradoxically, the more you hold the fort on that front and tame chronically uncivil behaviors, the more others will believe in your direction and want to jump on the bandwagon, which will naturally result in a reduction in overall resistance levels—and in the level of incivility overall.

Create an Action Plan

Like any other successful project, enhancing civility requires a solid action plan. The issues you will need to take into account as you plan are:

1. **The organizational context:** How do your plans fit within the larger values, goals and culture? What support might you require and how will you go about getting it?
2. **The team context:** To what extent is the team ready for change and how do you go about obtaining people's buy-in? Are there any team members who will be resistant and, if so, what action should you take?

3. **The work context:** What objectives and priorities are currently on the team's agenda, and how do you link the shift toward increased civility with these priorities?

4. **Your availability:** What are you reasonably able to do (really do, not just commit to doing and then shift your attention to some other priority) to lead successful change?

5. **Resources:** What resources, funds or aids will you require (for example, training, on-the-job learning aids)?

6. **Communication:** What do you need to communicate, when and to whom? What angle should you use to attract the maximum attention and cooperation?

Treat this project just like you would treat any other change: create a detailed plan, with realistic timelines and deliverables, monitor your progress, evaluate and change course as conditions on the ground unfold.

Enlist Organizational Support

You might be able to create the change you want on your own. If that is the case, go ahead. In many instances, however, it is beneficial to harness additional support that is available to you as a manager.

Your own manager's support might be useful and possibly even crucial. This is true especially when you're tackling chronic situations or uncivil people, as it might end up coming to your manager's attention in the form of complaints or union grievances accusing you of harassing or bullying the employee whose incivility you set out to tame. Your manager will be able to offer a useful perspective, point to potential pitfalls and commit to supporting you on an ongoing basis.

Other organizational resources such as human resources and employee or labor relations professionals might offer invaluable insights and strategies to help get you through. You can expect to encounter all kinds of challenges on this journey, so having access to as many perspectives and sources of assistance as possible will pay off in spades.

Make It Known that Change Is Coming

The human brain is more likely to notice differences and new patterns when it knows that such differences are about to happen. With this in mind, it will be highly beneficial for you to let people know that change is coming and what they can expect to see and hear in regards to such change. This way, as you begin implementing change in yourself and in the environment, they will notice those changes more readily and attribute them to the overall shift.

Furthermore, staff members have the right to know that they will be expected to live up to higher civility standards and be held accountable for incivility differently than in the past. The change should be perceived as just and fair. Let people know that you will, as a team, embark on a journey that will help boost civility. Use communication channels that best fit your context, such as an all-team meeting, written communication, one-on-one conversations or all of these. Pay special attention to those whose support of the project could be especially helpful, as well as those who might pose challenges to the process.

Specifically, consider including the following elements in your communication:

1. Outline the larger context as it relates to civility or lack thereof, including how the change connects with the organizational values and aspired culture.
2. Relay the business case for increased civility.

3. Explain why you are undertaking this initiative now.
4. Outline the process ahead—what exactly people can expect to change.
5. Discuss team members' role in the process ahead.
6. Affirm your personal commitment and how you will demonstrate it.
7. Own up to the role that your own behavior may have played in bringing things to where they are now (if you were lax in acting on uncivil conduct in the past, or you yourself have been uncivil, take responsibility).

Offer lots of opportunities for people to raise questions or concerns in any forum, and especially one-on-one. There will be some anxiety, even fear, and your job will be to help alleviate these feelings and encourage people to change.

Empower Bystanders to Take Action

If your team includes colleagues who are particularly uncivil, you will want to empower bystanders to take action to stop incivility in its tracks. Think of them as a silent majority of responsible citizens that needs to get mobilized. Empowering bystanders is always important but is especially so when you are dealing with incivility hubs within the group.

Bystanders find themselves in a challenging position. If they take action to stop the behavior, they are standing up for what is right, but the person being uncivil may not see it that way and may resent them, or even lash out at them. If on the other hand they do nothing, their silence (whether they intend it or not) sends a message that they agree with the behavior and even condone it. In such cases, the person who was negatively affected will feel even more isolated or upset, and the perpetrator of the behavior will feel encouraged to repeat it.

It takes courage for bystanders to take action, and they may feel unwilling or unable to do so. It is, therefore, important that you empower these folks to take a more active stance, even if all they do is use the "Let's not go there" phrase. That in and of itself will halt problem behavior. The more you are able to encourage and engage team members to take action when they are in the observer position, the stronger the team's civility fabric will be.

Launch Meaningful Dialogue

The more that team members feel a personal sense of responsibility for upholding a civil team culture, the less you as a manager will need to intervene and carry the responsibility for doing so. Furthermore, the more that they have a shared sense of what they want to create and why they want to create it in the first place, the stronger the civil culture will be.

Ongoing dialogue is one of the best ways to get people to share ideas and shift to a new way of being and doing in the workplace community. Through discussion in different forums, people can express their own visions, feelings and beliefs, and hear others express theirs. Through this continuing exchange, increased understanding emerges and new paths for action become possible.

Encouraging meaningful exchanges can happen in many ways. Earlier we discussed the advantages of creating team norms, where team members consensually agree on the standards of civility that will guide them. There are many other ways to elicit dialogue (many of which we've reviewed in this book), and you can choose those that are most suited to your particular context.

Provide Concrete Tools

You might find that your team members could benefit and gain competence in the civility arena if you equip them with tools and education, some of which you may or may not be able to provide on your own.

First and foremost is training, either live classroom sessions or web-based training. Some organizations, including Bar-David Consulting, offer on-the-job learning aids that equip people with skills that help them become more adept at modeling the right behavior and dealing with incivility effectively. Your best option is to find resources that are specific to workplace incivility, and offered by experts in this area. You can also consider using experts in the area of interpersonal conflict management, emotional intelligence or the handling of difficult conversations. Regardless of your choice, always take the time to ensure that you are engaging reputable suppliers and that you are getting into something that will specifically help with your civility-boosting agenda.

BUILD CIVILITY INTO THE TEAM'S DNA

Embedding civility into the team's culture will be exponentially more successful if you weave it right into its DNA. In other words, build the civility agenda into every step that a team member encounters throughout his or her tenure on the team: beginning with the questions you ask during the hiring process, continuing with what folks learn during the onboarding process and how civility expectations are communicated within the supervisory relationship, and building specific civility-related items into the performance appraisal process.

In addition, embed civility into the ebb and flow of team activities so that whatever is happening includes some aspect of civility awareness. For example, include it as an agenda item in meetings, whereby at the end of the meeting participants provide a quick 1 to 10 assessment of the civility level in play during the meeting (and allow time to discuss it if an issue is identified). Or assign a particular participant at every meeting as the person responsible for maintaining civility and flagging when attendees may be crossing the line.

Monitor the culture by introducing team pulse checks where team members have the opportunity periodically to share their observations and experiences regarding civility, or the lack thereof, over the past while. If the team is sufficiently large, you can use anonymous online surveys to harvest information in a confidential fashion and use the information to initiate meaningful team dialogue.

THE ROAD AHEAD

It may not happen in a day, a week or even a year, but once you turn your attention and efforts to boosting civility in the group that you lead, it will happen. And when it happens, the changes will be noticeable on many fronts. And you, I hope, will feel proud of the team and of yourself too.

IMPLEMENTATION CLINIC

Creating the Conditions for Success

Chasing the team culture is a project worth doing. A good action plan will help you succeed in increasing civility levels on your team. Reflect on the questions below:

1. What have you learned about implementing other team-focused projects that you can use now to make your change initiative successful? What are some do's and don'ts that you should follow when implementing the project?

2. To ensure that the initiative is successful, what types of support will be required?

	Objective(s)	Support Required	Required Action	By When
From your manager				
From human resources, employee relations or similar organizational resources				
From other organizational resources				
From external resources				

3. Consider the following questions and jot down your thoughts and plans in the box below:
   - Who on the team is already on board with regards to boosting civility and minimizing incivility?
   - Who is partly on board?
   - Who is not on board at all?
   - How do you ensure that the maximum number of people is on board? What action should you take to get them on board? What action should you take to leverage the support of those who are already supportive?

	Objective(s)	Support Required	Required Action	By When
Person A				
Person B				
Person C				
Person D				

(continued)

4. What do you need to do to empower team members to take action when they are in a bystander position?

5. What tools will you provide to the team as a whole to build competence in preventing and dealing with incivility?

* * *

CONCLUSION

My dear reader, our journey together has come to an end and now it is up to you to use the ideas in *Trust Your Canary* to be a better leader, leading a consistently productive and civil team.

Our journey took us from examining the definition and manifestations of incivility, through the business case for nurturing civility and into an exploration of the negative effects that incivility has on teams, organizations, your brand and even customer service. We considered why incivility persists despite the considerable damage that it creates, and paused to examine the underlying beliefs that enable it. From there we walked through various strategies and solutions, looking at the big picture as well as at the smallest details that can make a real difference.

Throughout *Trust Your Canary*, I have attempted to uncover many of the layers and complexities of workplace incivility. However, everything in this book is only the beginning of the story. The real narrative and the true complexities reside in your real-life work environment and within you. You are unique, and so is the team that you lead. You bring to the workplace individual histories as well as a rich story of working together in the past and present. All this requires you to be thoughtful and decisive as you move forward to boost civility on the team, to the benefit of all involved.

You are not alone. Despite the fact that our book-centered journey is over, I am here to help you in the future as well. Bar-David Consulting has developed additional tools to support you as you go forward from here, including a wide range of training programs, Respect-on-the-Go toolkits, learning aids for both leaders and staff, the learning hub on our websites at www.sharonebardavid.com and www.trustyourcanary.com, our free blog and more. I encourage you to visit our websites anytime for additional information, free resources, training programs and learning tools.

Contact me anytime at Bar-David Consulting:

Email: info@sharonebardavid.com
Tel: (416) 781-8132
www.sharonebardavid.com
www.trustyourcanary.com

Good luck on the journey!

SHARONE BAR-DAVID
Toronto, April 2015

ENDNOTES

1. This definition is inspired by the pioneering work of Christine Pearson and Christine Porath. They defined workplace incivility as "the exchange of seemingly inconsequential inconsiderate words and deeds that violate conventional norms of workplace conduct" (C. Pearson & C. Porath, *The Cost of Bad Behavior: How Incivility Is Damaging Your Business and What to Do about It* [New York: Portfolio, 2009], 12). Earlier definitions included: "Workplace incivility is low-intensity deviant behavior with ambiguous intent to harm the target, in violation of workplace norms for mutual respect. Uncivil behaviors are characteristically rude and discourteous, displaying a lack of regard for others" (C. Pearson, L. Andersson & J. Wegner, "When Workers Flout Convention: A Study of Workplace Incivility," in *Human Relations* (2001), 54(11): 1387–419.

2. *Merriam-Webster Dictionary* defines professionalism as "the skill, good judgment, and polite behavior that is expected from a person who is trained to do a job well."

3. O. Dotan-Eliaz, K.L. Sommer & Y.S. Rubin, "Multilingual Groups: Effects of Linguistic Ostracism on Felt Rejection and Anger, Coworker Attraction, Perceived Team Potency, and

Creative Performance," in *Basic and Applied Social Psychology* (2009), 31: 363–375.

4. K.D. Williams, "Ostracism: The Impact of Being Rendered Meaningless," in P. Shaver and M. Mikulincer (eds.), *Meaning, Mortality, and Choice: The Social Psychology of Existential Concerns* (Washington, D.C.: APA Press, 2012), 309–323.

5. C. Pearson & C. Porath, *The Cost of Bad Behavior: How Incivility Is Damaging Your Business and What to Do About It* (New York: Portfolio, 2009), 53.

6. C. Porath & C. Pearson, "The Price of Incivility: Lack of Respect Hurts Morale and the Bottom Line," in *Harvard Business Review* (January–February 2013), 1115–121.

7. C. Porath & A. Erez, "Does Rudeness Really Matter? The Effect of Rude Behavior on Task Performance and Helpfulness," in *Academy of Management Journal* (2007), 50: 1181–197.

8. Industries included food, beverage and tobacco, wood and paper, energy, chemicals, chemical products and textiles, metallic minerals and metal products, machinery and equipment, transportation equipment, electrical and electronic products, construction and related activities, transportation services, communications, finance and insurance, general services to business, government services, education, health and social services, accommodation, restaurants and recreation services, food retailing, consumer goods and services.

9. S. Bar-David, "The Incivility Risk: It's Time to Connect the Dots," in *Canadian HR Reporter*, October 10, 2011.

10. L.M. Andersson & C. Pearson, "Tit for Tat? The Spiraling Effect of Incivility in the Workplace," in *Academy of Management Review* (1999), 24(3), 452–471.

11. Based in part on C. Pearson & C. Porath, "On the Nature, Consequences and Remedies of Workplace Incivility: No Time for 'Nice'? Think Again," in *Academy of Management Executive* (2005), 19(1): 7–18.

12. C. Porath & A. Erez, "Does Rudeness Really Matter? The Effect of Rude Behavior on Task Performance and Helpfulness," in *Academy of Management Journal* (2007), 50: 1181–197.

13. S. Bar-David, "The Incivility Risk: It's Time to Connect the Dots," in *Canadian HR Reporter*, October 10, 2011.

14. C. Porath & C. Pearson, "The Price of Incivility: Lack of Respect Hurts Morale and the Bottom Line," in *Harvard Business Review* (January–February 2013), 115–121.

15. C. Porath & A. Erez, "Does Rudeness Really Matter? The Effect of Rude Behavior on Task Performance and Helpfulness," in *Academy of Management Journal* (2007), 50: 1181–197.

16. C. Porath & C. Pearson, "The Price of Incivility: Lack of Respect Hurts Morale and the Bottom Line," in *Harvard Business Review* (January–February 2013), 115–121.

17. C. Porath & C. Pearson, "The Price of Incivility: Lack of Respect Hurts Morale and the Bottom Line," in *Harvard Business Review* (January–February 2013), 115–121.

18. S. Bar-David, "The Incivility Risk: It's Time to Connect the Dots," in *Canadian HR Reporter*, October 10, 2011.

19. K.D. Williams, "Ostracism," in *Annual Review of Psychology* (2007), 58: 425–452.

20. N.I. Eisenberger, M.D. Lieberman & K.D. Williams, "Does Rejection Hurt? An fMRI Study of Social Exclusion," in *Science* (2003), 302, 290–292.

21. S. Bar-David, "The Incivility Risk: It's Time to Connect the Dots," in *Canadian HR Reporter*, October 10, 2011.

22. S. Bar-David, "The Incivility Risk: It's Time to Connect the Dots," in *Canadian HR Reporter*, October 10, 2011.

23. S. Bar-David, "The Incivility Risk: It's Time to Connect the Dots," in *Canadian HR Reporter*, October 10, 2011.

24. Definition inspired by Dr. Laura Crawshaw, in *Taming the Abrasive Manager: How to End Unnecessary Roughness in the Workplace* (San Francisco: Jossey-Bass), 2007.

25. O. Dotan-Eliaz, K.L. Sommer & Y.S. Rubin, "Multilingual Groups: Effects of Linguistic Ostracism on Felt Rejection and Anger, Coworker Attraction, Perceived Team Potency, and Creative Performance," in *Basic and Applied Social Psychology* (2009), 31: 363–375.

26. J.Q. Wilson & J.L. Kelling, "Broken Windows: The Police and Neighborhood Safety," in *Atlantic Monthly*, March 1982.

27. There were a number of changes Bratton instituted at the same time, including CompStat (a computerized mapping system to keep track of crime) and changes in incentives to police officers and police superintendents. The policing of disorder, or Broken Windows policing, was part of a package of changes made by Bratton.

28. Since that time, some researchers have questioned the extent to which Broken Windows policing in New York was the determinant factor in lowering crime rates. Despite some scientific controversy around the validity of extrapolating a cause-effect relationship between police actions and crime reduction, it is widely accepted that community action that is informed by Broken Windows Theory yields meaningful decline in crime rates.

29. C. Pearson & C. Porath, "On the Nature, Consequences and Remedies of Workplace Incivility: No Time for 'Nice'? Think Again," in *Academy of Management Executive* (2005), 19(1): 7-18.

30. K. Byron, *Loving What Is: Four Questions that Can Change Your Life* (New York: Three Rivers Press, 2003).

ABOUT THE AUTHOR

....

Highly successful organizational consultant and leading industry expert Sharone Bar-David has over twenty-five years of experience creating respectful and productive workplaces around the globe. A former family therapist and lawyer, Sharone's unique, comprehensive and human approach to tackling workplace incivility has made her a nationally renowned speaker and coach, as well as a long-standing contributor for *Canadian HR Reporter*. Her popular blog had gained a loyal international following. She is also a coach who helps transform the behavior of abrasive leaders. Sharone works in Toronto, Ontario, where she is President of Bar-David Consulting, a consultancy firm with a client base covering a wide range of industries and sectors. She is an avid yogi and the proud mother to daughter Leore, and strives to be an RHB (real human being) in all her endeavors.

Printed in the USA
CPSIA information can be obtained
at www.ICGtesting.com
LVHW092254291023
762506LV00019B/202